Analysts on Analyst Relations

The SageCircle Guide

ROBIN SCHAFFER

With Efrem Mallach PhD & Sven Litke

FOLROSE
PRESS

Analysts on Analyst Relations
© SageCircle, 2020.
First edition, 2020

978-0-906378-13-7 paperback
978-0-906378-14-4 ebook

Published by Folrose Press.

Printed in the United Kingdom by Lightning Source.

Table of Contents

Preface

Kea Company acquired SageCircle to help bring decades of carefully curated Analyst Relations knowledge to our clients. This book brings a voice to a global audience that is often missing from conversations on AR: the voice of the analyst.

> No two sages could be better placed to share this story than Dr. Efrem Mallach and Robin Schaffer. I've been honored to work alongside Efrem since March 2013, when he joined Kea through the acquisition of Lighthouse Analyst Relations. Efrem wrote the first book on analyst relations, 'Win Them Over', in 1987. The later editions of that book have made him a guide for generations of AR professionals. Robin and I met the following year through the Analyst Relations Forum, a series of conferences for the AR community which she helped lead. She, Efrem and the rest of the SageCircle team have unequalled experience in the analyst relations industry, having worked not only as AR advisors, but also as hands-on AR leaders in organizations like Honeywell, NICE and Unit4. As consultants, they are at the forefront of the AR community, working with some of the largest and most innovative AR teams. They stand far ahead of the static 'best practice' taken for granted by our clients' competitors.

Working together, Kea Company and SageCircle are helping our clients to increase the business value of analyst relations. Kea Company runs outsourced analyst relations programs using SageCircle's insights in two ways. First, the Kea Analyst Relations Portal has been a resource that has integrated and updated SageCircle's insights with the experiences of other firms acquired by Kea: Active Influence; Daruma and Lighthouse. Second, we practice what we preach by applying and developing SageCircle's leading-edge insights.

Along the way, we have had some remarkable successes together. We helped one of the fastest-growing business software vendors in history grow from a tiny start-up to a 'Unicorn' with a $10bn valuation using the guidance in this book. I hope you get similar insights from this publication.

Sven Litke, CEO, Kea Company

Foreword

As anyone who has ever been in a relationship with another person can confirm, knowing what the other person wants goes a long way to making a relationship run smoothly. That is as true of analyst relations as it is of any other kind. Your relationships with analysts will be better if you know what they want.

This doesn't mean you'll always provide what they want. Resource constraints, policy considerations, and the occasionally unreasonable nature of some analysts' "wish lists" make that impossible. However, knowing what they want is still a good jumping-off point. When you can do things equally easily in either of two ways, knowing which one an analyst prefers—or which one analysts of that type generally prefer—makes your decision easy.

In personal relationships, we have many ways to learn what the other person wants. We can observe their reactions to different situations, see what they choose to do when it's their choice, and more. Plus, of course, we can ask them what they want.

We don't have as many options with analysts. The nature of a professional relationship, as opposed to a personal one, limits what we can observe – but we can still ask them.

The problem with asking analysts what they want is twofold:

First, it creates an implied expectation that you will do what they ask for, or will at least try to. You can't avoid this. Asking creates an expectation, even if nobody mentions it and it's unwanted. However, you may not want to do what the analyst asks for, or may not be able to.

Second, you have limited time with any given analyst. There will always be many things to do in that time. Asking the analyst what he or she wants from you may not be its best use.

This book solves those problems for you. We asked analysts what they want, so you don't have to. We collected what analysts have said in a wide range of surveys over the years leading up to its 2020 publication. Robin Schaffer has organized them by topic and added "connective tissue" to explore and explain how they relate to each other and what they mean to you. The result is a deceptively thin volume that is all meat, no filler.

Read on!

Efrem G. Mallach

Introduction

Do you want to sway a whole industry and impact whether a vendor thrives or dies? Become an analyst.

Do you want to sway an analyst to help your company thrive? Become an AR professional.

Analysts talk to prospects, are quoted in the press, establish followings on social media, and frame issues for the market. All this means they are critical to a vendor's success.

AR professionals sit in the center of a complex web of information and relationships. We stand between the vendor and a highly influential, knowledgeable and opinionated audience of third-party experts. Mastering the art and science of AR ensures that you can have a huge impact on the future of your business.

Alan Petz Sharpe, founder of Deep Analysis, provides the analyst perspective on the AR role:

> I understand that AR professionals have a very tough job to do. Frankly, I do not envy your role. You have to try to keep everyone happy all the time, and that is an impossibility. I have deep admiration for many AR professionals. I have deep admiration for any technology vendor who stays in business more than six months. I suspect, though, that the vendors who really thrive in the coming years will be those that figure out how to relate to the marketplace – not just analysts – in a more transparent way.

Read every book you can about analyst relations by AR pros; there's great advice to be gleaned from the AR experts. But if our job is "relations," it is our job to understand analysts, and there is no better standpoint for that understanding than from the inside – the analysts themselves. This book is unique in that respect. It views AR from the analysts' perspectives – not ours.

The chapters that follow lay out varied opinions on standard practices in a field that is anything but. Different analysts have different business models, personalities, and preferences, so it is our job to listen, understand and respect their individual realities and needs. That is the only way we can engage them effectively and efficiently, and perhaps influence them to our benefit.

Ray Wang, founder and chairman of Constellation Research, puts the AR job in context and encourages us all to enjoy the ride:

> Being in analyst relations means you are in the middle of the action. It's fun! You see what's happening with the products and where the company is headed. You're privy to a lot of confidential information and there's a high trust factor. You're part of the team.

Analyst Relations professionals work in a wilderness. There isn't a map, or a recipe, and no single strategy that will guide us to the best possible outcome. We rely on our insights, instincts, and knowledge to influence the analysts and the companies we represent. 'Analysts on Analyst Relations' is designed to enable your success with insights from within and provide you a unique advantage for better analyst relations.

Chapter One

Analysts Explain Analysts

*T*he power of analysts is well documented. They can recommend you, cover you, inform you. They can enhance your sales funnel and elevate your company to new levels. And, if you handle them badly? Well, don't play with that fire. You will get burned and your company will get hurt.

Kevin Lucas, the Forrester analyst who covers AR, identifies the key objectives of a great AR program:

▶ Deliver business value

▶ Manage first-class execution

▶ Maximize analyst influence

▶ Secure needed investment

▶ Attain internal recognition of business contributions.

To achieve these goals, you first need to understand who and what you are dealing with. We'll start with some of the basics, then hear how analysts describe themselves.

Understanding Analyst Firms

There are three firms that dominate the AR industry, command the most attention, and employ the greatest number of analysts: Gartner, Forrester, and IDC. In order to start understanding firms, you must begin with their similarities and differences.

Gartner is by far the biggest firm, and therefore wields the most power. Gartner is the most powerful for two major reasons: they get 70% of their subscription revenue from buyers, and they keep a strong firewall between buyers and vendors to maintain strict impartiality. Notice I said "strict," not absolute; all analysts have biases, and it's our job to use those biases to our advantage.

Buyers (also referred to as end users) generally value Gartner's opinion. They will seek Gartner's advice for all sorts of issues, from figuring out the kind of technology they need in order to solve a problem, to identifying potential vendors, to selecting a shortlist, all the way to picking a winner and negotiating the contract. This is influence.

Gartner is geared towards IT and is strong with that persona, particularly in large companies. IT generally dominates the relationship with Gartner, but business decision-makers drive the requirements and participate. Not only does Gartner provide insights and recommendations, but their advice dispels FUD. The phrase, "Nobody gets fired for buying IBM," may have been the original adage, but in our field, it's "Nobody gets fired for buying what Gartner recommends." Gartner's Magic Quadrant is undoubtedly the most highly visible and impactful decision-making document in the technology industry.

Richard Stiennon, author of *Curmudgeon* (a highly-recommended book about the analyst industry) and a former Gartner analyst, shows how Gartner analysts can influence an entire industry through this story he tells in his book.

> Influence is the ability to impact a market. It is when your thoughts, ideas, and vision for the industry push the direction of the vendors and the adoption by end users (companies, universities, government agencies, non-profits, and consumers). At the very least, an influential analyst creates debate from her insights and declarations. That debate is one of the primary indicators of influence. It may appear in the form of bloggers taking you to task, journalists reporting on your contrarian views, even reporting in mainstream media on the consternation that your predictions or precautions have engendered.
>
> There are two primary ways to attain the heights of influence, the easy way and the hard way. The easy way is to have a platform from which to speak that, by your very position in the industry, people listen and react to. In politics this is evident when an elected official's opinion on something bears much more weight than all the experts in the world. Celebrities often demonstrate their influence.
>
> Many will recognize my story of how I had some small impact on the IT security space. It is worth retelling because it could only have happened because I was a Gartner analyst. When I joined Gartner in 2000 I was immediately assigned

the task of tracking the Intrusion Detection System sector. These IDS systems were generally software running on servers that would tap into the network traffic behind the gateway firewall. Lists of signatures were written that would uniquely identify protocol anomalies, worms, and network-based attacks. When the scanned traffic matched a signature, an alert would be generated and a log entry sent to a repository. After talking to hundreds of companies over three years, I realized that every single company I talked to was ignoring those alerts. There were just too many of them. Even Cisco, then the largest vendor of IDS products, had only a small team of five people working regular hours in their IDS group. Obviously, there was no great security value in something if you could take off weekends and holidays and be fine with that.

At Gartner's Security and Privacy Summit in June 2003, I made my big pronouncement, which was that there was no security value in IDS and Gartner customers should stop spending money on it. I advised that the money would be better spent on technology that actually blocked attacks. It seems obvious now, but back then Intrusion Prevention (IPS) was brand new. Three vendors are credited with inventing the new technology almost simultaneously, which is very common in most technology sectors; when it is time to invent something, the idea occurs to multiple entrepreneurs at once. IPS was the final reinforcement I needed to summon the courage to out an entire segment of my industry.

The Gartner press department took my words, and on the advice of my manager, Vic Wheatman, issued a press release that "IDS is Dead," which put a little sting into it. At the conference I spoke to a standing-room only audience. People were overflowing into the hall and watching me on a monitor. My big pronouncement was accompanied by a slide that said IDS SUCKS, and the audience applauded. You know that you have struck a chord when you get that kind of reaction. Besides, in the ensuing months many people sent me links to articles they had written years before saying the same thing, demonstrating the importance of the platform. This was not some IT security practitioner saying IDS was dead, it was Gartner.

As I walked away from the hall, the CIO of the Pentagon accosted me. He told me that he had heard me say this before and it was high time I came to the Pentagon and addressed his key IT managers. After the physical damage caused by a plane crashing into the Pentagon on 9/11, they were spending huge sums on revamping the networks inside the rebuilt Pentagon, and they had budgeted $160 million for IDS. I told him to name a time and I would be there.

Within a month I was being escorted through the Pentagon to a conference room. On the long walk, the Colonel escorting me said, "Oh, by the way, we invited some other industry experts to the meeting." These other industry experts were the founders and CEOs of all the IDS companies. I had been invited to a debate.

Apparently the only real impact I had on the Pentagon was to change a single letter, D (detection) to P (protection), in the Pentagon's Requests for Proposals. But the lasting impact was that the IDS vendors made great strides in moving from noisy sensing solutions to proactive defensive solutions.

Gartner may be the biggest and most influential firm in the industry, but it is just one of many. Forrester has a similar model and approach. Like Gartner, Forrester sells subscriptions for research to buyers and vendors, which provide access to analysts for research and advice. Similar to Gartner, Forrester sells most of their subscriptions to end users. Forrester concentrates its research and commentary on technology-related business problems, while Gartner's research and analysis is deeper and more concentrated on the technology itself. Forrester's signature report is their Wave, a vendor evaluation that is very influential and dominates in certain spaces. Like Gartner, Forrester is respected for their impartiality, and their opinions are considered highly credible.

IDC is also in the top three. IDC is larger than Forrester in revenue and analysts but has a very different model. Their strength is in the numbers. IDC has data that analyzes trends, market shares, industry forecasts and more. As a result of this, IDC is highly valued by the media and the firm. They expect their analysts to be heavily quoted. IDC focuses more on the vendor side, with less direct impact on buyers, and their research is respected as impartial. IDC has much more international coverage, with analysts in most countries. These analysts are broad rather than deep, knowing the local technology trends across the market. The company is noted for being easy to work with, and for its many offerings that help with message amplification.

So, we start with the top three, but there are 1269 other known analyst firms. These are firms of all sizes, down to individual analysts. Many are boutiques, focusing on specific technologies, regions or verticals, with a variety of approaches and business models. They can be focused on market data, user surveys, or thought leadership, and many are 'sell side,' serving vendors who have an insatiable thirst for market data, third party validation, competitive intelligence, amplifying messages, or feedback on their products, marketing, and services. Fewer are 'buy side,' serving end users who need advice on technology decisions. Most of the buy side firms also serve the sell side, erecting a Chinese wall to keep the parts of their business separate.

A major firm outside of the top three is Omdia. In February 2020, Omdia brought together 450 analysts from former firms Ovum, Heavy Reading, Tractica and the majority of IHS Markit's technology.

Roy Illsley, Chief Analyst at Omdia, talks about life at a firm fighting to be one of the big three. From Illsley's perspective, Omdia, 451 Group, and Analysys Mason are all challenging Forrester to be in the third position.

> Based on my experience as an end user years ago, companies had two subscriptions – Gartner and one other. The CIO subscribed to Gartner, but it was too expensive for everyone to have access, so most users had the other. It gave us another perspective. When the CIO said Gartner suggested X,Y, and Z, we'd have another perspective. If the two firms disagreed, it would be a project for someone to go out and find the real facts.

> At Omdia, we bring a unique value proposition to the market. Subscribers (about 70% vendors and 30% end users) get the combination of strategic advice from senior analysts with market data, forecasts and end user surveys. We help vendors make decisions on where they should be going, what they should be doing, how they should be marketing themselves. as well as the detailed data in terms of their relative positions in the market, and what their strengths and weaknesses are by comparison to their competitors. For end users, we provide the research, maturity models, and advice on strategy and implementation. We're looking to grow our end user base. In terms of influence and customers, we're not as strong as Gartner. We've got some work to do.

> Traditionally, we have been very strong serving the EMEA and APAC market with lots of expertise on the ground, but we didn't have enough analysts in the US. We now have a good number of US-based analysts throughout the country, so we find it easier to get enterprise buyers by having more resources in their time zone that know and understand them.

Daniel Newman, founder of Futurum Research, describes the changing role of analyst firms and their influence on buyers. Smaller firms capitalize on these changes.

> The modern analyst is a lot different than the 10 year ago analyst, and what companies need in an analyst is a lot different. Essentially, there was a time when the analyst was a highly specialized person that tended

to have deep expertise in a very narrow space. They understood the entire landscape, all the players, and was a trusted advisor. They worked directionally - either towards the vendor or towards the user, and those two things were generally mutually exclusive. Now, the analyst has a hybrid role where they are the trusted advisor through mass media, because the way people consume has completely changed. A lot of the buyer's journey is pivoted, and the analyst journey has as well.

The buyer that used to want a trusted person is now reading articles, white papers, infographics, watching videos, listening to podcasts, and so the analyst has been forced to have a depth of knowledge, but also to be an influencer or a media personality that can reach markets and make markets.

We've built a business based on the idea that they don't just need people that can understand the technology, but resources that can reach important stakeholders– shareholders, buyers and media.

I just think it's a very different business. I think the independent firms are never going to be able to compete by trying to do what the Gartner and IDC do. We need to compete on adding greater values at higher levels in the organization.

Robin Bloor provides a view into how some firms provide consultancy and the influence on buying decisions.

An analyst does technical due diligence, provides product development consultancy, does benchmarks, does surveys, does communications testing, reviews marketing collateral, writes sponsored white papers and sits on the advisory board providing advice on anything and everything.

If that's their whole life, then you might want to hire them - if they're very good at any of these things - but you have no great incentive to make sure they're up-to-date on your technology. You don't need to target them in the hope that they will pass your message on. The people they're most likely to explain it to are your allies or your competitors.

But if an analyst spends any time working for users then they may be passing your message in some way to potential customers. They might be doing one of two things for such customers:

⊘ General consultancy

If my experience is anything to go by, general consultancy will most likely involve strategic advice on major projects. These projects usually involve briefing the customer on products, but only as part of the activity. The reason an analyst has been hired is because he or she will know a lot more about different options, because they know an awful lot more about different products than your typical consultant. Analysts also get retained by companies so that they can provide advice of this kind on a regular basis.

It can be a breath of fresh air for the customer, because the typical analyst is not forever trying to introduce an army of additional consultants into their company. An analyst may also try to provide the best practice advice.

✔ Product Selection

What vendors fear most is that an analyst will be called in to provide product selection consultancy and will mention their product unfavorably; or, just as bad, not mention it at all. It's a sensible fear, but the reality of product selection exercises that I've been involved in is that I have never had much influence over which product was selected. All I influence as an analyst is:

- ✔ Which products get on the selection short-list.
- ✔ How the evaluation is carried out.

The analyst is hired primarily to ensure that the selection process is coherent, and to provide information to the process as it proceeds. The shortlist normally includes the dominant vendor if there is one, plus two other vendors whose products most closely match the requirements. Even if the dominant vendor's product is a poor fit, they get onto the shortlist so that no one can say; *"You mean you didn't consider Oracle? Are you crazy?"*

In many cases, which product is selected doesn't matter too much as long as it can do what it claims to do. Bad product selection occurs when some salesman makes unjustified claims:

User: *"Can it scale to 10,000 users?"*

Salesman: *"Hey, can jumbo jets fly?"*

Be warned. That's an example from real life – and as it happens, that particular jumbo jet couldn't fly. The analyst is there to stop such travesties.

Understanding Individual Analysts

To build a great program, you have to go beyond the firm and understand the individual. Each analyst has a specialty, even within the same firm. Some analysts care about the products, some care about the quarterly results, some care about the strategy. This is part of the profile you build about all the analysts that are important to you. You have to know their research, their point of view, and also something about their personal interests, like the name of their dog.

Ray Wang gives a view on how to delineate among analyst types. He looks at who is influencing the market, who can really dig in with you on the product, and who can amplify your messages.

▸ The first type is by their market orientation. Are they client advocates on the buy side, doing contract negotiations, advocating for their clients? They primarily take the client's point of view.

▸ Product strategists are second. They are the ones that know the product needs in depth. They may have been in the industry for a long time, so they can provide guidance and direction.

▸ Then there are market evangelists, who can go out and actually take a topic and tell a story through the media.

To stand out as an analyst today, you have to meet two out of those three criteria. That enables you to provide the most value to the clients.

Brian Sommer, founder and president of TechVentive, talks about the difference in the knowledge and influence of analysts. Some really understand the market, have real world experience, and tell you honestly how it is.

To understand a good analyst, you need to understand the way wild animals find game. They look for silhouettes – that's what catches their eye and their attention. A good analyst knows the trails that companies and executives operate on. They're not that terribly new and different, and they're fairly consistent. So they have a pretty good idea about a vendor from the trail of breadcrumbs they leave.

In my experience, the best analysts spend a lot of time with customers – actually getting down in the trenches and helping with selections and implementing. So when a vendor says they have a truly global product, the analyst can call bull based on their experience that it only works in two countries, and even then they can't even get it to work in one of them. The analyst can stand firmly on first-person knowledge and experience. That customer-facing experience helps them recognize the patterns over time.

A vendor can spot one of these analysts. The ones that spend time with customers or have had decades of experience in the space will call bull in a heartbeat.

Robin Bloor shares his view of how analysts in an industry sector support each other through a "virtual circle."

As an analyst, I believe it is my duty to try to understand how technology will evolve. When I come to a conclusion on this in some area, I write about it. Sometimes I get it wrong and sometimes not. I'd rather be right than wrong, because quite a few people take note of my opinions. I don't just want to understand how technology works, I want to understand how the industry works. I don't fully understand it, so I need people to teach me.

There's a Japanese proverb that says; *"You may be cleverer than any one of us, but you are not cleverer than all of us".*

It is not to be taken too literally. When it came to physics, Einstein really was cleverer than all of us. Giants happen. But that's not the focus of this piece of wisdom. This delightful little proverb tells us that knowledge is usually dispersed among a group, and if the knowledge of a group can be harnessed, it can be very impressive. That, IMHO, is what an analyst should be doing; gathering and harnessing the knowledge of a group. But which group?

After being an analyst for 10 years, I concluded that there was "a virtual circle" within the IT industry, a group of individuals, who truly understood the industry or at least some part of it. It wasn't a club that you could join or that met anywhere. It was just a virtual circle of talented men who, collectively and informally, moved technology forward. Some of them knew each other, and even if they didn't know each other, they recognized each other when they met.

These were the people I wanted to meet and interact with, because I could learn from them. And so, they were the people I met with whenever I could. How to recognize such people? It's easy; they know what they're talking about.

When I encounter any member of the "virtual circle" I do a lot more listening than talking – and when I talk to them, I get them to criticize the way that I frame things or represent ideas. I do everything I can to pick knowledge from their pockets.

I doubt if other analysts see it exactly like that, but I suspect it's the same for many of them (unless they're saddled with an unfortunate ego, which insists that they already know everything-and-his-dog). They want to meet and exchange opinions with people that know. They want to connect with the virtual circle. If you are in AR and you enable that for any given analyst, they will be grateful.

And if they're not, something's wrong.

Tiering Analysts

Stop! Wait! There are 7,500 individuals who consider themselves analysts. There may be hundreds relevant to your space. Each has aspirations, preferences, a personality, and a way they make money. You can't know and treat them all equally. Don't try. It is a mistake - a big one, a common one, a waste of time and resources, and guaranteed to minimize your effectiveness. You must prioritize analysts and manage them accordingly. Tiering analysts according to their impact is critical to your success as an analyst relations professional and running a program that has impact.

The analyst tiers are separate from the firms they work for. You'll hear Tier 1 associated with the big three, but you need to do this on an individual basis. There may be a Gartner analyst who only tangentially touches your space and is Tier 3, while a one-person show may be a mover and shaker in your industry and goes on the Tier 1 list. Don't be blinded by the impact of a firm; look at the impact of the analysts themselves.

A general rule of thumb is:

▸ **Tier 1** — The most important analysts. No more than 10 per company or business unit. These analysts you will engage with in depth. Lots of one-on-one time, inquiries, strategy days. You'll understand their perspectives and have regular goals to make them more and more positive.

▸ **Tier 2** — The next level of importance and relevance. About 35 per company or business unit. These analysts need to be in the loop. Some may have one-on-one briefings and inquiries, but you'll handle engagement as efficiently as possible. Group briefings and webcasts help you reach this audience.

▸ **Tier 3** — The analysts that are relevant, but are not a focus. About 100 per company or business unit. Use newsletters and other broadcast communications to stay in touch. You want them to know your name and key messages.

Don't be rigid. Do be efficient. Don't overthink it. Move individual analysts from tier to tier depending on changes in their focus, your company's goals, and your mood, shirt color or horoscope. The goal is to prioritize your efforts.

Understanding and tiering analysts is never easy. There are several dimensions:

▸ Level of influence, both direct sales impact and market influence

▸ Coverage area

▸ Regional focus

Ray Wang talks about understanding an analyst's influence.

> When you're tiering firms you're trying to figure out who influences the buyers – are people going to buy from me because of them? The tier process comes into place based on how influential you think these analysts are with whatever stakeholder you're looking at – partners, customers, the press and media.

Robin Bloor digs more into the process of identifying who is influential. It comes down to research.

> AR professionals know how the larger analysts companies work (and if they don't, they shouldn't be working in AR). However, even if you didn't know, you could easily work it out. If you have a large number of analysts, you have to organize them so that they specialize in specific technology areas. They can then earn revenues according to that specialization by producing research, writing white papers, doing consultancy or whatever.

> So if you represent a company, you can find out who you need to talk to in the larger analyst companies simply by ringing them up and asking. But with the smaller companies, you don't even know whether you should be talking to the company at all and if you think you should, then you won't necessarily know who in the company you need to talk to.

> You need to find out!

> Bear in mind that what you are trying to find out is: who are the influencers in our market?

But how do you find out?

I'm hypothesizing that you are running AR for a promising technology vendor and you want to know which analysts you need to impress. In my opinion, you cannot actually buy that information, because no one I know of specifically stores exactly that information (with the possible exception of some of your competitors).

So what do you do?

Here's a novel suggestion: behave like an analyst and research it. Surf your competitors' web sites and read their press releases to see which analyst or analyst companies get a mention. Google "your technology area" + "analyst" and also get a Google news feed with those two terms together. Enter your technology area as a search item on analyst web sites. Ask the journalists that cover your area which analysts they speak to about it. You might even ask some of the analysts you know who they respect (some will help, some won't, but if you don't ask, you don't get).

Be creative. Be open-minded. Don't use one measurement or criterion to identify which analysts are influential. You might ask your sales team who they see involved in deals. You may want to directly survey your customers. Can you ask incoming leads as part of the qualification process? How about including analyst involvement in win/loss reports?

Know your analysts. Understand how each analyst fits in the landscape of influencers. These steps are essential and foundational for building a great AR program. And don't forget a hearty breakfast. It takes time and energy up front to create a program that works for the long term.

Chapter Two

The Influence Landscape

There is a broad landscape of influencers in the enterprise market. You may be responsible for many or all of them. It is critical to understand how each one fits into the big picture. Each influencer must be categorized and then managed appropriately to your best advantage.

In addition to analysts, members of the influence landscape encompass:

- **Journalists.** This includes trade press and general business press. They are often overwhelmed and in search of a good story to boost their reputations and readership. The care and feeding of journalists differs from that of an analyst. They don't have the depth of knowledge, so information needs to be higher level. Let them know why your story is important to their readership. Find the angle that links to readership, and you and the journalist have found a common goal and will be working together on spreading your story.

- **Bloggers.** Blogs have broad readership and, like analyst research, they can have a broad influence on the marketplace. Bloggers impact vendors. Key bloggers must be identified and relationships managed. Some of them are analysts, but many are independent thought leaders. Buyers consider them, so you should, too.

- **Consultants.** Like analysts, consultants have a strong influence on buyers. Some are also analysts, some only consult. If they write, their papers are influential. Get to know them and get them to know you.

- **Academics.** Scholars in ivory towers conduct in-depth research and often impact the direction of the industry. Vendor involvement with academia can be very powerful.

- **Associations.** Industry groups for particular verticals or technologies have members who study and buy technology. They look to the association for guidance on direction. Associations often host events with vendor sponsors. Partnering up with these associations enables you to participate in industry leadership.

▸ **Customers.** Users who advocate for your solutions are extremely powerful influencers. Prospective buyers listen to their stories – positive or negative. Their impact goes beyond the sanitized case study. Your company's next customer will take a past customer's story as fact and consider any disasters as predictive. Customer influence is in conversations, social media comments, and peer reviews.

As you peruse your market of influencers, make sure your company has a plan to leverage each type. It is often a shared responsibility, or owned by colleagues. But AR has a strong voice in the influencer strategy. Use it.

Journalists

Treating analysts as journalists is a very common mistake, both by internal organizations and outside PR agencies. Robin Bloor explains how you need to treat these audiences in different ways.

Within their Marketing and Communications departments, large IT companies have both Analyst Relations (AR) professionals and Public Relations (PR) professionals. Note that they are not usually the same people.

One obvious reason for this is that analysts and journalists are distinctly different in what they do and why they do it:

✓ An analyst is a domain expert and a journalist rarely is.

✓ An analyst is often also a technology consultant and a journalist rarely is.

✓ Journalists produce information for the general reader of their publication. Analysts produce information specifically for professionals in their coverage area.

✓ Vendor companies hire analysts for specific assignments but almost never hire journalists (except possibly for presentation work).

Why does any of that matter?

Those facts matter for several reasons. PR professionals can do AR work, but unless they have experience in it, they are likely to irritate the analyst by doing such things as:

● **Sending press releases.** Analysts are only interested in a small number of press releases (if any) and are very sensitive to information overload. They will treat regular mindless press releases as spam and they will think less of the company that issues them.

● **Arrange senseless briefings.** All analysts could spend all year doing nothing but getting briefed. If you arrange a briefing for them, it needs to be worth their while. If it isn't, they will think less of the company and/or product.

Bloggers

James Governor, co-founder of RedMonk, talks about the role that bloggers play in the landscape.

Bloggers and non-traditional analyst firms are influencing technology and product strategies. In order to make money, many of the blog influencers will try and make their way as paid trusted advisors. Some will do implementation work as well. They influence the market.

This is both a threat and an opportunity for "traditional AR" to define its roles and responsibilities.

Governor points to different types of bloggers, such as RedMonk itself, to demonstrate that a blogger has the power to influence industries, especially technical communities. He talks about others who may not take paid gigs, but give important advice via PR channels like conferences. Publishing networks create new stars and influence models. And some independent vendor bloggers can elicit trust, even though they work for a vendor.

He continues on with the power of networks, and the importance of true, ongoing engagement.

I suspect that the nature of trust is changing, as it becomes based on networks rather than large companies. This is not to say classic firms don't have a role to play, but transparency is leading to some different ways of quickly establishing trust. Prejudices tend to show, like dark hair through blond roots.

Of course in this world, personal branding becomes more important, while judgements about relative authority become somewhat more subjective. New skills are required by influencer management organizations and professionals.

One of my favorite sayings about blogs is that they are about being "famous for 15 people." If these readers are the right people that influence can be profound. But how do you formalize that? Qualitative analysis becomes more important.

The critical point about any influencer program is understanding influence as a lifecycle. Treating PR, AR or consultant relations as a pure outbound marketing function is certainly the wrong approach. Those that can foster a dialogue, be prepared to get out of the way of the transaction where appropriate, but ensure the feedback loops keeps turning, and be in a good position to be a successful influencer manager. You need to learn to work multifaceted webs of influence.

Consultants

Richard Stiennon covers the consultant role and its distinction from analysts.

Many of the same traits are shared between analysts and consultants. Often consultants are subject matter experts and they are usually great presenters and even good writers. But the business models and their contributions are completely different. The typical management consultant is a generalist who can quickly adapt a set of tools and processes to a new challenge, be it a restructuring, process improvement, or strategic engagement.

Consultants have intense, often long-term interactions with their clients. There is a lot of interviewing, compiling, and frankly regurgitating in the consulting business. Industry analysts on the other hand are acknowledged experts in their space. Their research into industry practices turns into their base of knowledge, which they share with clients on demand.

A typical engagement for an analyst lasts a day, not weeks. The analyst listens to the client's presentations on their current practices and tools and the issues they have identified. The analyst then draws on his or her extensive knowledge of hundreds of similar organizations and spells out any deficiencies, or opportunities for improvement. The first encounter with an analyst can be refreshing or abruptly shocking. A consultant asks questions to help him or her get up to speed on your industry. The analyst asks questions that allow him or her to judge the maturity of your technology deployment. What is the makeup of your staff? What tools do you use? Have you investigated these other tools? The analyst will then simply tell you what you should do.

Many people have never had an opportunity to experience this type of interaction with an analyst. Their perception of analysts as pundits and pontificators is based on seeing the analyst present or reading their research reports. As a neophyte analyst at Gartner, I went along with a senior analyst on a day trip to a startup in the secure file transfer business. I had the technical background to participate as I had helped another such company with an end-to-end security review of their offering. This veteran analyst had worked with dozens of startups. His questions and hard-hitting guidance struck me as well worth the huge fee Gartner charges for such strategic engagements. Now, after seventeen years as an industry analyst, I too have worked with hundreds of technology startups. I can see their future and the decisions they will have to make in the ensuing months as if their timelines were already charted before my eyes. I can immediately identify issues with their go-to-market message, their sales and channel strategy, and holes in their talent pool. As they present, I usually jot down a dozen opportunities for them to partner with other vendors, or candidates to sit on their boards and generate business opportunities, or resellers that would be interested in their products, or investors that have expressed an interest in their space. Of course, an analyst shares all of this information and holds nothing back. The engagement fee has already been paid and they are there to earn that fee.

A consultant would be aghast at the idea of giving away all these golden nuggets of wisdom at the first meeting! Instead, they would hold back, sketch out a plan of attack, and contract for as long term a project as possible.

Understanding all the players and their influence enables your company to manage each appropriately. To optimize your plan, next we look more into the value that analysts and vendors provide to each other.

Chapter Three

Mutual Value – Vendors and Analysts

*A*nalysts and vendors have a complex relationship, but they share a critical stakeholder – the buying customer. The vendor is selling widgets. The analyst is selling advice on widgets. And whether they are in alignment or disagreement over the quality of that widget, the customer is in the middle. As AR professionals, it's our job to make it a dance, not a tug of war.

Analysts and vendors need each other. Analysts depend on vendor information, experience and perspective as critical inputs to their industry knowledge. Vendors need analysts. A positive review by an independent third party can close a sale. Insights on the marketplace can change the course of a vendor's plans and products.

The AR professional conducts, regulates, and creates the flow of information between the vendor and the analyst. It's our job to create value for both sides of the equation, your company and the analysts. A win-win has long term value. Don't just ask what the analyst can do for you. Ask what you can do for the analyst.

Analyst Value

AR pros are well-schooled in the value an analyst can bring to a company and applying this value for impact. But the analyst perspective on this adds the specifics.

Rachel Happe was an industry analyst with IDC and now runs a vibrant community of business leaders focusing on better audience engagement. From her experience at IDC, she shares how analysts can add value to vendors.

▸ Because of position, analysts hear and see more than most other people in a market; we are hubs and the better we synthesize information (and that depends on the analyst), the better insight we provide for corporate strategy, product planning, marketing strategy, and marketing communications.

▸ Also because we are hubs, we can introduce people. Call it old-fashioned match-making but we typically know senior managers and they are likely to respond to our introductions.

▸ Press and financial analysts like a third-party perspective. If you want your message put in a larger context we can often be helpful – whether that is in general or for a new product release. We cannot, however, help much if you just send press releases to us. The more we know, the better we can put your strategy into a larger context.

▸ Frameworks, data, and trends: This can be useful for market messaging, market strategy, product planning, corporate strategy, and sales training.

▸ Acting as an external team member that can review and comment on plans.

▸ Using the visibility of the analyst to get attention – this is highly dependent on the analyst

Mike Guay, a former Gartner analyst, explains the impact analysts can have on customers.

Gartner analysts speak to hundreds of customers a year across various verticals, using various software systems. This gives analysts a broad perspective of customers' needs and concerns, as well as the strategic aims of their organizations. This knowledge is valuable to vendors seeking advice, because it provides a real-time view of the market and an independent data source to compare to their own market research.

This works both ways, as the more communication analysts have with vendors, the better information analysts can provide to the analyst firms' customers. Analysts are often asked to confirm rumors regarding vendors and their products. The larger the fact base, the better quality the advice. The influence of analysts is very strong. Combined with years of industry experience, the background of discussions with customers and other vendors enables analysts to communicate with vendors at depth about what their existing or potential customers are considering.

The Gartner Magic Quadrant report has a huge impact on buyers. Although vendors and customers alike tend to focus on the leader quadrant, analysts are adamant that readers speak to the authors of an MQ before making a buy decision. It helps to provide background to potential buyers about where vendors are positioned and why. For example, if a vendor is in the niche quadrant, it may be because they only play in certain verticals or certain geographies. Yet a Niche vendor can often be a great choice for the right customer.

What do analysts want from vendors?

In AR, we generally make assumptions about what analysts want and try to deliver it to them. But nothing beats their own perspective.

Many years ago, a highly influential but unnamed analyst published this list of wants.

1. Spending a day consulting with a vendor on strategy

Most analysts find tremendous value in these types of interactions and no, it's not what you think – it isn't because the firm gets paid for these days, or in some cases because the analysts get a "spiff". It is because they know what you should know. That by spending eight hours or so with somebody, you get a much better picture of who they are, what they do, how they do it, where they are going and how they are going to get there. You also have a much better chance of furthering a relationship at the same time.

2. Receiving written case studies that have not been published by the vendor

Use your "customer capital". Great case studies are worth their weight in gold. Offer the case studies and be prepared to back them up with customer references.

3. Receiving competitive information or vendor comparisons from the vendor

This one is surprising. Although the analysts don't value where you rank yourself vs. your competition, they do value who the vendor "calls-out" as competition and where they spend their cycles in differentiating themselves.

4. Speaking at vendor-sponsored events/seminars/user groups, etc.

DMBs typically get paid for these activities, and our research shows that these activities don't inherently impact analysts' position on the vendor. Where these can show a big impact is in enhancing relationships.

5. Presenting competitive analysis to vendor's sales force

Though frequently given from stock presentations, competitive analysis and comparisons give the analyst an opportunity to conduct research as they present.

6. Being a press or media reference

Much different from being asked for a quote, being used as a press reference is actually encouraged by many analysts. The gating factor is their understanding of your company & products, as well as the depth of your relationship with the analyst.

7. Being asked to speak at a vendor webcast

The least valuable speaking engagement in the analyst's eyes. They find less value and more hassle with webcasts than other types of venues.

8. Receiving vendor white papers or positioning papers

Analysts are increasingly finding well-written, non-marketing hype, internally developed white papers valuable to understand the vendor's strategy. The key here is INTERNAL. Don't give them white papers for hire from some quasi analyst.

9. Analyst conference sponsorships

Though many analysts will exhort vendors to exhibit at conferences, conference sponsorship does not impact their opinion of a vendor.

10. Having reports reprints purchased and distributed by vendors

Most analysts don't find value in vendors buying and distributing their research. We think this comes from the generally low level of emphasis analysts put on research (as opposed to inquiry).

11. Having vendors provide help with finding speakers for conferences

Most analysts would rather find their own speakers, and resent vendors trying to place speakers. However, if you asked this question of the event managers at the analyst firms, you would get a far different answer, and it would include cash!

12. Being invited to supply industry-oriented quotes for press activities

Most DMBs HATE being asked for quotes – especially for press releases. Gartner analysts can't give them; the others may or may not, depending on their mood. If it's a quote you want, you'll need to turn to a second-tier analyst. Most of the DMBs will not provide industry quotes on behalf of a vendor.

13. Being asked to write a white paper by a vendor

DMBs hate being asked and REAL analysts won't do them anyway. There are other sources of getting your marketing collateral written.

The late Jon Toigo, who was a major analyst in the database storage space, responded with his own point of view. His riff off the original list shows us what other analysts really want.

#1 — spending time with the vendor — is generally a good thing for the reasons articulated. You get to know people and to assess how smart folks are and whether they have the capability to execute on plans. I like doing this, especially when someone picks up the tab for the flights, hotels and restaurants. I should also point out that I get a feel about a company based on their logistical provisions. I would rather stay at a nearby two-star hotel than a far away five star. I can fly coach comfortably for up to two hours. I am not impressed by food. (Frankly, the best meals I have had are a little chain restaurant in Dallas that serves all-you-can-eat soup and salad. The bill is usually a whopping $10.)

#2 — unpublished user accounts — I generally do not want these. Just point me to your customers and I will chat with them myself.

#3 — competitive comparisons — I like these, not because they are always accurate, but because they clue me in on what the vendor is trying to say is important about his product. Plus, you can get some great issues to follow up.

#4 — speaking engagements — C'mon. I will take any bully pulpit I can get. So long as I am not gagged by the need for political correctness or censored about my views regarding the vendor's products or its competitors'.

#5 — presenting to the vendor sales force — same as above. I want sales guys to know what I am hearing from the trenches just like I want consumers to know what's going on in vendor land.

#6 — being a press reference — the press shouldn't be talking to analysts. They should be talking to vendors and consumers. I am happy to give an opinion, which is like an arsehole: we all have one. If I were a consumer I wouldn't give a rat's ass what any paid analyst has to say about any product.

#7 — doing webcasts — same as 4 and 5. I want to broadband, lowband and highband.

#8 — receiving internal papers — I read voraciously. Send me everything that you think is important and I will read it.

#9 — getting sponsorships — I want to put on a show now and then. I want vendors to pay for it. I also enjoy turning down unscrupulous vendors who want to sponsor. My way of saying "Frack You."

#10 — having vendors reprint and distribute reports I've written — Delighted, if they are so inclined.

#11 — having vendors provide speakers for conferences — Only if the vendor is proffering something visionary or smart, then only from the vendor's organization (and usually only if I am impressed with his/her communications capability, so I am reasonably sure he/she won't put my audience to sleep)

#12 — providing quotes — Delighted to under the terms identified in #6. (But unlike other analysts, I don't charge for this.)

#13 — writing whitepapers — I do it all the time. Writers write.

In addition to being an excellent analyst, Toigo had additional skill as a humorist. Let's take a short break for his snarky additions.

▸ Tell me all of your product problems so I can share them with your competitors and appear smart and hire-worthy.

‣ Offer me a job that will get me out of my pay-per-view job and give me a shot at some real money.

‣ Give me a lot of money or stock so I can buy a new car/house/wife/girl on the side/etc. and show how much more important I am as an analyst than my competitors.

‣ Give me big public awards and laud me for my brilliance. That way, I can compensate my ego for all the stupid things I am otherwise saying for pay.

Commercial Relationships

Money is an interesting subject. Ask most vendor executives and they'll tell you that analysts are pay-for-play and if you spend enough, they'll rate you well. But that's hogwash. Those who really know the game understand that any analyst who advises buyers, or any analyst with scruples would never taint their reputation with vendor bias because of money. Does every analyst have scruples? No. Be wary of any that offer to support all your messages and position you as a superstar for a buck.

Mike Guay gives us the real scoop on whether Gartner is "pay for play."

> Gartner analysts sometimes hear that large vendors who spend a lot of money get preferential treatment. This is not true. I can state unequivocally that Gartner analysts are very objective and agnostic, and the primary focus of analysts (I believe at all analyst firms) is to provide the best advice to our customers regardless of vendor spend.

> I think what happens is that larger vendors will allocate a significant amount of resources to interacting with the analyst firms. This means analysts get a lot more information than they might get from one of the smaller firms. While frequent vendor interactions may have an indirect influence, there is no causal relationship between vendor spend and preferential treatment. Most analysts don't even know what a particular vendor spends with Gartner.

Constellation Research has buyers as their main customers. Ray Wang says this:

> Our team doesn't care about a vendor's spend because it's the coverage area that they're interested in. I don't think the revenue from vendors matches the level of coverage. In fact, the revenue from certain technology areas is low, but we cover it because the information is in demand from

our customers. We write first and if the vendor wants reprint rights, they can buy the reprint rights. It has no effect on our coverage. We cover vendors in market views and shortlists all the time and we never ask for money. If you want to do a video after with us, that's up to you. There are a lot of things like that that we do because we're supporting the buy side. The attitude towards vendor revenue depends on your firm's business model. If you have buy side clients you have to be unswayed by vendor spend.

Dan Newman has a different perspective. As a sell side analyst, working 100% with vendors, he finds challenges in balancing the revenues they deliver from the opinions the analyst shares with the market.

> As an analyst, our job is to inform and educate, and sometimes what we're going to say will be contradictory to what you want us to say, but that is also what gives us credibility. If everything we say about the brand is always positive, we look more like a shill than an analyst. Some AR teams no longer want honesty, they just want promotion, and there is a big difference. I think that can be managed by having good communications with the company for negative perspectives. We talk through it and if the analyst still thinks there is negativity that needs to be communicated to the market, at least you've shared it with them. You do the best you can.

Longtime analyst Lawrence Gasman talks about the interesting dilemma of AR teams who are both influencing the analyst and funding the analyst:

> One of the things that hurts relationships between us and analyst relations managers is that they are often the same people who decide which firms they will purchase research from. So on one hand they are positioning their company to us in the best possible light, and on the other hand they are holding the purse strings for potential research budgets. There can be an incentive to not buy research from firms that have said anything negative about them. This is not a good situation ethically. I just think it would be better if analyst relations could be separated from the purchasing function for everyone's benefit.

Rik Turner of Omdia, presents how trust in a vendor is affected by commercial projects.

> The issue of trust comes up when I do a white paper or webinar for a vendor. They lose my trust when they try to control the message. I appreciate that since it is something they are paying me to do, it needs

to generally support them, but I lose respect for vendors that want me to write what is essentially their marketing material. They don't have a view of the value of an analyst giving an objective view of what is going on in the market. Even worse, if I am writing a regular research report and they indicate up front they want to buy distribution rights, some vendors expect to dictate the content that I'm writing. That's just silly. All they're really doing is paying me a lot less to write marketing copy than if they went to a marketing agency. That ruins my credibility and tarnishes the whole industry. There are one or two analyst houses that will do that and they negatively affect us all.

Find the win-win between the analysts and your vendor. It will help your program bring utmost value to both. It is an art to play both sides of the street without getting run over, but as AR pros, that's the game we chose to play. When you find the right balance, your AR program will win for all.

Chapter Four:

The Analyst World

*W*e're all busy. But no matter how busy you are, analysts are probably busier. Imagine a chipmunk with ADD and a caffeine addiction. That is the person whose attention you are trying to grab and whose opinion you are hoping to modify. Individual practices and business models will vary, and understanding how analysts work helps AR pros to position ourselves properly and engage analysts productively. We are professional diplomats developing relationships. In this section several analysts provide a view on what their day and life looks like. Understand the person you're about to call. It helps you strategize your approach.

Jeremiah Owyang, founder of Kaleido and formally a Forrester analyst covering social networks, provided this during his days at Forrester.

> Apparently the role of an industry analyst is shrouded with mystique and misconception. Meeting the many folks that I interact with online is much different than meeting them in person. In fact, people are much more candid and honest with me in person, and certainly over a beer or two.
>
> At least once a week, people tell me "I could never do what you do, being stuck doing all that data crunching". Apparently, the perception is that industry analysts spend most of their time sifting and sorting long spreadsheets. While that's actually some part of my job, it isn't the entirety.
>
> Following is a list of how I actually spend my time. I'm certainly only speaking about my experience, and by no way am reflecting on the experiences of others.
>
> Pay myself first: Every morning, for about 2 hours before the world wakes up, I spend time reading everything I can on my industry,

books, blogs, articles, reports. I use this time to manage my blog, manage comments, look at who's talking to me or about me. You'll often see a flurry of tweets as I link to things that I think are interesting. If I stopped blogging, I would continue to get paid, but I know the value of being part of the conversation, both personally, professionally, and how it helps me in my day job.

Use the tools I cover: I come from the trenches, and I've always found that the best way to understand tools (and more importantly, why they matter) is for me to use them. I push the tools to the limit, break them, then report back on how to effectively use them (or not at all). You'll often see that I am often asking questions, spurring on discussions, and teasing out insight. If you haven't figured it out, you are all in my lab, not as test subjects, but as co-scientists.

Research: The most important aspect of my job as an analyst is to conduct research. I've a research agenda that is based upon the feedback of clients, as well as where we think the market will need help. I need to spend quite a few hours a week obtaining data, adding feedback to the surveys and other data collection tools we do, conducting interviews, and simmering the content into something tangible and real.

Presenting/sharing: I often present my findings from research at conferences and on webinars for clients. It's important to share what I've learned. The product is educating those who want to learn more.

Helping Clients: This is the area of the day job I'm most passionate about. Perhaps the most unknown fact about my job is that I spend time helping clients. I act as a high level advisor, provide guidance, or can dig deeper into consultation projects, or can even bring a team in to help companies. The end result is helping business leaders make the right decisions.

Briefings: This is more of the 'input' that fuels my research. I've been briefed by many companies in my coverage space and I'm getting to know my market better and better. I honestly have a hard time keeping track, it's overwhelming.

Press Meetings: Another output is that I share my findings and insights to the press, who are seeking a third party opinion. I'm contacted by reporters all over the world who ask me for findings, data, and opinions on the area that I'm covering.

Industry Events: You'll frequently see me at Bay Area tech events a few times a month. it's pretty easy as there are about four tech events every night in Silicon Valley.

Rachel Happe chimes in with the various responsibilities she had as an industry analyst. Here she shares her likes and frustrations.

▸ Writing: I write roughly 40 documents a year, 15+ of them major documents

▸ Research: Surveys, interviews, and participating in online discussions

▸ Presentations: 6+ presentations at conferences and briefings

▸ Modeling: Forecasting and developing systems models to mimic market behavior

▸ Briefings: I'm going to estimate that I've taken 150+ briefings from companies (and I turn away many)

▸ Inquiries: 2-3 a week from buyers, Wall Street. firms, VCs, or big services firms

▸ Customer Events: I've probably been to 15-20 of these events

▸ Customer Projects: White papers, presentations to internal groups, or strategy days with senior product, marketing, or M&A teams

▸ Talking to the press

▸ Responding to emails, scheduling, returning phone calls

▸ Talking to prospects, preparing proposals, preparing surveys, cleaning data

▸ Program development and planning

▸ Program marketing: collateral, sales training, etc.

▸ Collaborating with other analysts

What is great about that job:

✅ To access such a diverse cross-section of market influencers: vendors, buyers, investors, and press and with it the opportunity to see so much.

✅ Endlessly interesting – the conversations I have and the people I meet and work with are a great part of the job…goes along with "Never a dull moment."

✅ My colleagues – I've been learning a huge amount from colleagues who have seen the rise and decline of markets.

✅ The flexibility to prioritize where I spend my time and what research to pursue.

What frustrates me:

- The expectations that I can grow a new program, write extensively, get visibility, and manage the administrative side of my job...and be human. I feel a little set up to fail and I don't like that. Granted most of these expectations are my own.
- The limited ability to explore new business models – I'm a start-up girl and I'm used to being able to experiment.
- The craziness of all the things that I do feeds my ADD (no, not really) which is not always helpful.
- I'm a doer and I like developing a product with a team and seeing its evolution - I'm disconnected from that as an analyst.

Richard Stiennon explains the reality of being a Gartner analyst, which is perceived as being quite prestigious, but the reality is starkly different.

There is surprisingly little support structure at Gartner—no research assistants, secretaries, fact checkers, or Business Intelligence tools to help them. There is a huge staff of editors but they are often a hindrance, not a help. Gartner editors make sure that Research Notes are in the "Gartner voice," thus eliminating the opportunity for an analyst to imbue his or her research with his own voice and flavor of discourse. Gartner analysts are individual contributors and remarkably free from the day-to-day hassles you would expect from a highly paid professional, often with the title of Vice President. They have no direct-reports, thus no employee evaluations to fill out, and few meetings, except by conference call to discuss research agendas and coordinate Summit activities. They work from home and are often on the road. Other than producing Research Notes and presentations, the vast majority of their time is taken up with briefings and inquiries—predominantly over the phone.

The analyst expresses their opinions and objectives by creating deliverables, such as research, blogs and white papers. Our goal is to align the analyst's opinions and objectives with our company's. Let's go over the channels analysts use so we can better understand exactly what we are trying to influence.

Research

Research is a core element of analysts' work. Reading what they write informs you of their thinking about the market, products, technology models, and more. This window is your opportunity to bond with the analyst over what they care about, and position your company in the analyst's mind.

Mike Guay explains the research process at Gartner.

> In the large firms like Gartner, there is a lot of structure about how research is conducted. This can be helpful in providing a consistent quality and content in written research, but sometimes leaves less flexibility and creativity to the individual analyst or analysts. However, the size of Gartner means that we have a very broad and deep set of internal expertise. The internal exchange of expertise and knowledge can lead to excellent research and inquiries.

> Gartner has a process where an agenda manager works with other analysts and executives in the firm to determine the agenda for the coming year. This is enumerated in the Primer reports for the various agendas. This is often informed by strategic research such as the annual technology trends report and trends in the area of analyst coverage – ERP in my case.

> Once the topics are defined, the practical experience as an analyst and input from hundreds of inquiries helps structure the research. This often includes a formal definition of the relevant technology, capabilities, limitations, and what customers should be expecting to see from vendors. The most important objective is research that provides value to our clients.

Mark Smith, CEO and Chief Research Officer at Ventana Research, details how his firm defines topics.

> When we decide on research to develop, we take big bets on markets where we believe we can shape the conversation. We have had great success defining markets like Integrated Business Plans, 13 years ago, and Sales Performance Management, 17 years ago. We make bets on categories that we believe directly align to buyers. We do things like search LinkedIn for people with emerging job titles and follow them to see the interest in a market and the changes over time. For example, we were talking about subscription management and we looked to see how

many business professionals have the word subscription or subscriber in the titles. Turns out there are 185,000. We watch these trends. We make sure our research is aligned to the folks that are part of the subscription management movement. Three to four years ago, AI and ML were the topic of conversation, and we found 440,000 people. Now there are 22 million people with that in their job title. It's a movement and we have to be aligned.

Once we understand a movement, we use primary research and qualitative methods to find out exactly what is going on. If you don't do that you're just pontificating from the corner office with opinions. All our analysts have 30 years of experience in the industry, but we all agree that we're not as smart as the collective wisdom of the movement. I see an analyst firm's research and methodology as an aspect of its brand value. We put a lot of energy into that.

Blogs and Social Media

Most analysts are very active in the blogosphere and on Twitter, LinkedIn, etc. In the last 15 years or so, these channels have worked together with more formal research and subscriptions.

Ray Wang, lead for Constellation Research, and one of the most visible analysts in the industry, says this:

> There is a lot of obvious value in blogging and social media. They help your brand and make your company a bit more famous. All research, even with a good report behind a paywall, should be amplified in social channels to get the word out. There is so much information out there and social media helps you cut through the noise and go direct to the audience.

> The paywall plays an important part in the analyst firm model. Paywall research is typically unique and specialized information. People pay for access to it and vendors pay to reprint it. The analyst industry depends on the paywall model to exist. But if the analyst's research covers a critical topic to buyers and supports the vendor's message and nobody knows you wrote it, nobody cares. The balance between all that is social media because it gets the commentary and concept out into the market.

Social media is misused if the analyst only sees it as a broadcast tool. These are engagement platforms, and a good analyst uses it that way. We use it for polling, to reach out to clients, to share things that our clients are doing. About 60% of our buyer clients are in social media. We see it as a full on multi-modal communications tool.

White Papers

White papers are somewhat of a conundrum. The biggest firms don't do them; some that do them aren't reputable. Avoid temptation. As indicated, a small percentage of experts will say anything for money. Steer clear of them like your career depends on it. Long range, it does. Your challenge is to find the reputable analyst that shares your perspective. Opinions vary. You'll find one.

The third-party perspective, when respected by the readers, helps amplify and validate your messages. A strong customer case study becomes even stronger when presented by an independent party. Make sure that party is reputable, credible, and independent. When money talks, it's time to walk.

Robin Bloor describes this.
There are two aspects of white papers that I think deserve some comment. The first relates to why a vendor would ever invest in one and the second is about how they should be designed, written and produced.

Let's begin with the commissioning of a paper. Basically there are two possibilities:

- Vendors will license the use of all or part of an existing analyst paper because they like what it says and because they feel that it fills a hole in their array of marketing materials.

- Vendors want to be able to distribute a custom written paper that meets a perceived marketing need. And so the paper is commissioned by the vendor.

The first of these "white paper products" – the licensed extract – is untainted by the suggestion that the vendor has simply persuaded an analyst to write it "to order." It is possible that the analyst company has produced a biased report of some kind knowing that a particular vendor will want to pay a license fee for it, but that's unusual in my experience.

I produce many product comparison reports and we never know when writing them whether any vendor would be likely to pay a license for reprints. It's actually quite difficult to know ahead of time what any vendor will think of your white paper. For that reason, primary research is rarely deliberately biased. (Bias usually stems from incompetence and is random.)

The situation with commissioned white papers is distinctly different. The analyst company and the vendor need to tread very carefully if they intend to produce a useful piece of marketing material that serves them both.

There are four types of commissioned papers:

- ◉ The Puff Piece: Some vendors seem to think that getting an analyst company to write something highly complimentary is going to serve them well. The problem is that it won't serve the analyst company well (unless it specializes in such work) and most readers will see it for what it is.

- ◉ The Thought Leadership Piece: This is a white paper which focuses on describing a business problem that can be solved by a specific piece of technology, possibly also explaining the nature of such technology in detail. This need not mention any vendors or products and can simply be presented by the vendor with other marketing collateral with the implication that their products and/or services offer the appropriate solution.

- ◉ The Thought Leadership Piece with Product/Service: This is essentially the same as the above with the added nuance that the vendor's product or service is used as an example of a solution. This could be interpreted as a puff piece by the reader, but will not be if the product/service is just accurately described rather than extolled.

- ◉ Case Studies and Best Practice: Papers which are essentially case studies have the benefit that the reader can read the details of how a particular technology was used and the kind of "best practices" that need to be employed in implementing it. Such papers can be very effective because they tell a story of how a problem was solved and hence help the reader to conceive of how a solution will work, in terms of effort, methodology and time.

Naturally there is a wide variety of structures that can fit in around this. There are "green papers" which involve a number of interviews with customers using a specific technology that is then turned into a paper. It has a number of brief case studies but also includes some statistics on which particular business resulted from the use of a particular technology. This may include a few explanatory pages about the technology. Sometimes a single brief case study may be added to a thought leadership piece to provide illustration.

White Paper Usage

Usually white papers are available as downloads from the vendor web site (in exchange for potential customer details), may be handed out as part of a webinar, and will normally be printed and distributed at trade shows. Additionally they will form part of the rep's sales pack and should be available internally within the company as they can also help with staff education. I can think of three examples where papers I've written have been distributed internally for education purposes. They all involved the launch of relatively new products, so staff needed to know what the company was up to.

In summary, the targets of a white paper are buyers, influencers, partners/channel and internal staff, and there is no reason why the same white paper would not hit all targets. However the prime target is the prospect. The goal is simply to bring the prospect closer to engaging with the vendor by:

- Positioning both the company and technology – showing where it fits in.
- Indicating which business problems the technology solves. (Technology either cures pain or creates opportunity and may do both).
- Providing explanations of how the technology works and why it addresses the problem.
- Providing indications of proof of concept (case studies and technical explanations both contribute)

Despite your initial impression, analysts are people, too. Each comes with different interests, different skills, different strengths and an assortment of weaknesses they prefer not to admit to your face. Your mission is to design a program that takes advantage of the individual strengths of each person on the best team you can assemble. We do that by taking careful measures of the talents, focus, and influence of each analyst we enlist.

Analysts cover many areas, but they do specialize. Evaluate each analyst's focus and work product to get a sense of how best to achieve your overall mission using the mutual values your company shares with each individual. Someone who spends most of their time on research may not be a good speaker. Someone who specializes in white papers may not give you the competitive feedback you need..

So far we covered the analysts, the influencer landscape, value, and the activities analysts do. If AR is a game, you just learned the rules, the pieces, the board. Congratulations. You're about to actually play the game. It's time to learn strategies.

Best Practices for a Great Relationship

A great AR pro knows that working with analysts can make or break a company's reputation. Ignoring them is obviously wrong, but so is addressing them the wrong way. You need a clear vision of your goals and your approach with each analyst. You need a clear strategy that brings the right resources into play with the right analyst at the right time. Never engage just for the sake of engagement. It's a waste of the analyst's limited time, limited patience, and good will, if such good will ever existed to begin with.

When your goal is to influence an analyst's thinking so they, in turn, can influence buyers, your goal is a tough one. There is no switch you can flip to change an expert's mind. It takes a lot of hard work over a number of months or even years. It takes careful planning, thoughtful execution, and a coordinated, sometimes company-wide effort. Make sure all your stakeholders are committed to the size and scope of the task you all need to undertake.

When engaging with analysts, there are various modes to consider – from you to analyst, from analyst to you, and interactive discussion.

▶ In the first mode – from you to analyst – you inform them about your company, your strategy, your products, etc. This happens in one-to-one briefings with Tier 1 analysts, one-to-many engagements with less critical analysts, and through email and press releases for minor news and updates. These activities are generally orchestrated by the AR team.

▸ The second mode – from analyst to you – gives you the market trends, statistics, competitive intelligence and end-user insights you need to ensure your company advances. The market intelligence or strategy group is usually involved to leverage the insights. This mode almost always requires investment in subscriptions and data services

▸ Finally, interactive discussions. These can cover a wide range of topics of mutual interest. Analysts love this. They love being the authority and seeing their wisdom applied. Discussions of this manner require a commercial relationship for the biggest firms, but small ones often appreciate the opportunity to chew the fat on trends They will engage to a degree with no money changing hands.

These exchanges certainly can give you information and insights, and at times you will find their value enormous. When you engage in this type of dialogue – especially when led by your top executives – it will enhance the relationship significantly with your Tier 1s. With the exchange, you engage on a whole different level and raise your position in the analyst's mind. Do this right and you will impress and differentiate. Do it often and you will be memorable.

As the AR pro, you are the connection between all parts of the organization and the analysts. To the analyst, you are the eyes and ears and link to the smartest minds you have. Facilitate a holistic, two-way, continuous dialogue.

Great AR

The biggest differences we see between good and great AR is the insight the AR pro has about the analyst's specific interests and coverage areas, and the ability of the pro to facilitate the right connections in the organization and build those relationships.

Alan Pelz-Sharpe starts us off with a list of great insights about working with any analyst firm.

Twelve Do's and Don'ts

1. Don't assume the analyst is out to get you.

You are not as important as you may think. The analyst is writing about many vendors, so you are just one in a long list. You almost certainly have no context to judge their review of your product, in light of what they have said about your competitors. You may wish to consider slowing down before jumping to bias conclusions. In my most recent report, the AR group that had the biggest and nastiest hissy fit was the vendor that has received one of the more positive reviews in the report.

2. Your reputation precedes you.

The aforementioned vendor was also the vendor that had the biggest hissy fit last time they were reviewed (different product, different report, different analyst, same comprehensive treatment). They are also the vendor that analysts from rival firms share AR horror stories about. The firm has decent enough technology, but a terrible reputation for bullying or attempting to coerce analysts. That might work with some analysts, some of the time, but not all analysts, all of the time. Perhaps even more importantly, analysts learn over time which vendors and vendor staff people can be trusted to tell the truth (the whole truth, and nothing but the truth) – and which ones can't.

3. The technology customer is king.

If the analyst's methodology is focused on talking to customers and partners and you have been asked to supply customer references, respond in one of two ways: politely but immediately decline, or do your best to provide references. Ignoring the request for weeks or months is not a good policy and will only arouse suspicions rather than put the analyst off the scent. By that time, customers and partners have been found by the analyst and interviewed. When critical views are captured from such interviews, you should not at the last minute claim "our customers love x or y or z!" We know they don't, and frankly you haven't been able to supply any that do. Harsh as it sounds, we are not just going to take your word for it.

4. Don't threaten analysts.

If you don't like what an analyst has written, try at least to be respectful and polite. You are far more likely to enter a dialogue that way. Provide real facts to counter their critical assertions; if you cannot provide facts and instead rely on bluster, you will only dig a deeper hole for yourself. Also remember that analysts are human, threats via nasty e-mails (the coward's way) or phone calls can backfire, and they don't get forgotten quickly. Using such a confrontational approach does not make the AR person look important or even imperious, it makes you look unprofessional.

5. Don't quote your own press releases or other analyst reports as evidence.

There is frankly nothing sillier than to tell an analyst that they must be wrong about your firm/product because "Forrester/Gartner/IDC...ranks us as a 'leader,' etc." The only thing that rivals that is to quote from your own press releases. Trust me, this happens all too often. Most of the time, this kind of response will simply result in an internal e-mail chain that shares the joke with other analysts. Bottom line: this kind of supporting evidence looks desperate, patronizes the analyst, and suggests you have simply drunk too much of your own Kool-Aid.

6. Never say "we provided an X% ROI to our client in less than six months, etc etc."

It's a silly thing to say, period, and a particularly daft thing to boast to buyers. It's a little like Home Depot claiming that they dug my vegetable garden for me, when all they did was sell me a spade. You provide tools, people use the tools, and using those tools provides business benefits (or doesn't). And just like the spade I bought from Home Depot, remember that we all know most software likewise goes unused.

7. Don't kiss my ass.

Flattery will get you nowhere. Neither will generous offers of fancy meals, drinks, flight tickets, five-star hotels, (none of which many analysts can accept anyway), or the other perks that are stock-in-trade of influencing influencers. If you respect my work, do us both the favor of playing it straight.

8. Don't ask me for advice.

This one sticks in the craw of some vendors. They'll say: "but I spent all this time with you and gave you references, and you won't return any feedback?" Here's the deal: advice to a vendor from an analyst that advises buyers constitutes a conflict of interest. Any advisor to you will become invested in your success, which is good for you, but bad for the analyst's credibility and future objectivity. Just as importantly, it's not fair to other vendors. We are observers and critics, not market-makers.

9. A demo should actually demonstrate something.

AR people love to talk about their software, but are sometimes reticent to actually show it, or reluctant to show it under conditions reflecting something close to a normal enterprise environment. I think the revolving door between vendor product managers and industry analysts has helped to legitimize a culture of "briefings" completely via PowerPoint. Static slides can certainly identify the ever-beloved product strategy, but will fail utterly to convey the real experience of using an interactive application. And as we get into the demo and I ask you to show certain things and answer deeper technical questions, then...

10. Make sure you understand how your product works.

Or include someone in the conversation who does. A dirty secret in our industry is that many product and marketing managers are mistaken about how their product actually functions. Or they swear that a feature they spec'ed in actually made it through a rushed development and testing period...when in fact it was left on the engineering floor without anyone 'fessing up. Some of our more interesting moments as analysts have been pointing out to irate product managers that their own documentation or demo contradicted their marketing claims. All the more reason to...

11. Understand the difference between a fact and an opinion.

For every ten vendors I evaluate, there will be two that freak out. With the other eight we agree to disagree, and where there are errors (I make many, and do my best to fix them) we work together to get them corrected. I never want my reports to contain factual errors, nor do you. But my opinions are my opinions, I am paid to have opinions. To change my opinion requires a very different approach from AR. To change my opinion you need to understand why I have formed that opinion (see below) before attempting to "re-educate" me. In addition, when you claim a report is full of factual inaccuracies, and then send an annotated Word document listing differences of opinions – and can quote no factual errors at all – expect your response to be ignored.

12. Understand that customers implementing your systems have a very different perspective to share.

Just as I will view your product or service differently than you, recognize that a channel partner, a user, an implementer, or a consultant will all have differing perspectives. We base our evaluations primarily on what implementers experience. When a report does not reflect your personal or corporately-mandated vision, that does not mean it is wrong. Remember, if the only research you have read is from people you directly or indirectly pay, then it won't be surprising if you find some kind of uniformity with your own viewpoint. True outside opinions will by definition differ from your own.

Extra Credit: Don't believe your own hype.

We know it's your job to be passionate about your company, about its product, and its services. We understand it's your job to help sell this vision and to educate us all. But make the effort to really understand your competitive landscape too. Don't live in a vacuum. Analysts don't. I applaud your enthusiasm, and I wish you and your colleagues the best of luck, but I wish all your competitors the same too. I am not passionate about your company, I am passionate about ensuring that buyers and users avoid costly and sometimes disastrous mistakes. I want them to pick the right product each time, and use it to their best advantage. To the extent that's your goal, then we have the same agenda.

Having been in the industry for 10 years and having run research practices and undertaken extensive competitive intelligence, I am well aware that the vast majority of "traditional" analyst firms are dependent on vendor funding of one form or another to pay the bills, and that clearly flavors their dealings with and reporting on vendors. It's the way it is – whether I like it or not.

Chris Perrine of G2, long-time analyst firm sales and marketing executive, shares his perspective of what to avoid.

▸ Delays are always a challenge. "Nos" are sometimes better than "Yeses" if there is a sizable chance of a delay, and if it's a "Maybe," give a percentage chance.

▸ Smaller analyst firms often have challenges getting facetime and AR does not take the time to understand the smaller firms. They often cover areas the major ones neglect, and they can provide more focused attention on their key areas.

▸ Vendors have a lot of requests – briefings, events, other calls – and analysts also need time to produce research. It really helps to provide a schedule or any other heads up to help analysts focus and prioritize.

▸ Vendors often only offer one-way streets. They want to tell you A to Z about but will seldom help with research. Analysts really appreciate the relationship and benefits of a two-way street.

▸ Lack of humility. Tell the analyst what you're bad at. Show what you're working on. Be candid and go off-script. Ask "what else do you need?"

He goes on with some "tips from the trenches."

▸ Ask analysts about their upcoming research agendas. "What one report can we provide you the most help on and what can we do to assist you?"

▸ Work with the analyst firm sales team – their interests are aligned with yours. Don't view sales as the enemy – they can often be huge enablers to your work with their firm.

▸ When looking for an analyst, start with a broader search and then become more refined (especially in markets like Asia Pacific). Don't start with "I want a CRM focused analyst who knows Banking & Finance with knowledge of Asia Pacific". Start with what's most important to you - CRM, Banking & Finance, or Asia Pacific and then try to refine your analyst search from there.

▸ Don't call smaller firms "Others." Call us something unique like Independents, Up & Comers, etc. Smaller firms cringe when they see themselves lumped into this category.

Dan Newman shows the value when AR relationships are prioritized and executed well.

> Great AR teams are responsive and give you availability to the right people. Great vendors have folks committed to AR that have the bandwidth, the capacity and the relationships within the company to actually put you in front of the right people. When you have questions, they give you information on a timely basis. They are proactive vs. reactive. They get you briefed often and give you information so you are early to know, where you can then be that expert that's got early market opinions. AR becomes a trusted resource, and I become a trusted resource to the media.

David Wilson, analyst at Fosway Group, puts AR into perspective for a European-based firm.

> AR people need to have an understanding of what analysts are really about and what analyst relations is really about. They have to be clear on their motivation to engage and build a plan relevant with the right analysts. They need to be structured and proactive about what they do, but also to listen and tune into what the analyst says.

> There is a complete spectrum of vendors. We deal with the big software vendors who have got AR very defined. I would argue that they have a rigid approach to their process. They are largely gatekeepers and they try to control the narrative. They're ostensibly a facilitator, but can easily become an obstacle. You have to get past them to talk to people within that vendor who are actually quite keen to engage with you. We're never going to be a Gartner or Forrester, but in Europe in our space, we are quite influential.

At the other end of the spectrum are very small companies who don't have a clue about Analyst Relations. You typically deal with somebody in marketing whose views around the way analysts work is quite distorted or even non-existent. They are focused on basic marketing goals. It takes time to build a relationship with them and to recalibrate the way that they view it.

There is a sweet spot where the vendor understands the analyst role and has the right motive to engage. That is a combination of both listening and trying to amplify their message or create influence externally. They see the influence on the buying process from vendor evaluation reports like our 9-Grid.

Ritu Jyoti, analyst from IDC, explains how great vendors change her mind.

An important way for a vendor to change my view from negative to positive is to bring me the people and information that prove that you know the technology and the market. Bring me the experts who can go deep on the technology, not just the marketing story that says you are the best without the substantiation.

A vendor can change my mind when they show me vs. just talk about what they're doing. Take innovation. If a vendor has a reputation for not being fast and innovative, and they tell me their story in a very cohesive way, bring in their research team, tell me where the incubation of the idea happened, show me the customer and partner involvement – that will change my mind. I need the details and proof points.

Sometimes a vendor conference can change my mind. If they are a start up, but put on a greatly executed conference filled with customers and partners speaking for the product, experience, the value and impact, that will substantiate them and show them as more mature than I might have thought they were. I can see that they are really doing things.

There are many styles of AR, and James Governor provides some insights to what he considers great. Any team can excel with the right understanding and focus.

Often AR people complain about resources. But I see that the size of the team is a mark of the seriousness with which a vendor treats AR, rather than being resource overkill.

Certain vendors are world class because of solid execution, not because of the number of bodies on the team or the amount of money it spends. While other vendors whine, 'but we don't have the resources to deal with a wide range of firms", great AR teams just get on with it.

Great vendors put senior management executives in front of RedMonk or other small firms, not just my pals at Gartner. Thanks. When you're taken seriously you take the other party seriously. The simple truth is that there might not be a RedMonk if it weren't for the willingness of big firms to support us.

What makes an AR team world class to my mind is that it's set up as a listening organization, rather than a broadcast/bombast organization. More bodies are required because AR is about relationships. While other vendors aim for control of message, great AR aims for influence of message – that is a fundamental difference. Broadcast and command and control models for AR ignore all those opportunities to learn from a community of pretty smart people. The Big 2 have no monopoly on insight, IQ or experience.

Dan Newman speaks about the trend for AR to be heavily influenced by the PR mindset, and how that can negatively impact your relationship with an analyst.

I think the biggest thing that I've seen historically is this mega shift from AR and PR from being these two very separate things, to being much more of one and the same in a lot of ways. Analysts are being more and more forced to withhold candor at times to maintain the business relationship. A lot of firms make you feel that if you tell the market that you don't like something they're doing, that you don't believe in their product, or you think the company's strategy is poor, you're at risk.

We're seeing PR become an increasingly influential component to any relation strategy. PR will come over to AR and complain that the person AR works with (you) just wrote a really bad piece about the company on Market Watch... and then AR will call you up and ask why you are saying bad things about them.

Asking the analyst

Every relationship is different, but every expert – including Drs. Ruth, Phil, Oz, and Sage Circle – agrees that one element is the key to success: Listening.

Don't expect to apply the same strategy to every analyst. Ask directly and respectfully how to best work with them. Then listen closely and adjust your strategies accordingly. Analysts will appreciate the consideration. You will increase your influence. Your boss will approve of your effectiveness. Dr. Phil won't yell at you. It is always best to ask, listen, and act accordingly.

Wendy Nather, who led 451's security team, gives us some insight on working with analysts that is always an AR debate. Many vendors invest in niceties to try to sway an analyst. Some can respond to this, but others are indifferent. It is important to know who you're working with.

> Extravagant swag, parties, etc. don't make a difference. I've had dinner at Michael Dell's house; it didn't change how I analyzed Dell's offerings. Just be friendly, respectful, and honest.

Robin Bloor adds his perspective on knowing the analyst firms and individual analyst to know how to best engage with them.

> Analysts arrive at their own opinions and you cannot stop that happening (unless their opinions are for sale, in which case they don't really have opinions; just open palms). If one of them concludes that your technology is inferior or that your company is flaky, then you really need the relationship. If you don't have a relationship with the analyst, you have no chance of limiting the damage from that. You may not be able to change his or her mind, but you may be able to get them to tone down their message.

> A long, long time ago I published a report which slammed the Oracle database. Oracle's marketing staff in the UK weren't sure how to deal with it, because it was definitely costing them business. What they decided to do was exactly right. They called me in and did their best to forge a relationship with me. They made sure I was briefed on every new Oracle development. After a year or two they even hired me to give the odd presentation.

> They neither tried to bribe me, nor to silence me, they just established a relationship and gave me as much attention as they could. They gave me their point of view and I listened. They did not try to argue me into submission.

> There is no sense in arguing with an analyst. You may as well try cutting water with a sword.

As an AR pro, you're a matchmaker, therapist, business strategist, internal advisor, in addition to the eleven other hats that you wear. Your role is critical. Your impact, huge. The next chapters delve into the art of analyst engagements, the interactions that are critical in developing relationships and influencing the influencers: briefings, inquiries, strategy days, events, and executive meetings.

Chapter Five:
Briefings

You engage with analysts by applying the different types of engagement to the goals you have for that analyst. In this chapter, we'll cover the most common form of engagement: the briefing. Vendor briefings contribute greatly to an analyst's overall impression of your organization. Simple steps can help you improve the desired impact.

A briefing is like theatre, a show you put on for an audience of one. First, determine what story you want to tell. Like all great theatre, the briefing has a beginning, middle and end. The pace that the story unfolds is critical. Assess where your company stands with the analyst and what you can reasonably change before you write your script.

▶ An analyst new to you or your space needs background on the company – history, vision, financial performance. General market position for your company or new product is very important to include.

▶ Analysts want to know your view of market trends and drivers, and how they affect your clients and organization. Tell them your target market, your differentiators and your ability to deliver.

▶ For product updates and new products on the market, be sure to provide the level of technical detail that matches their coverage and interest. Some want all the speeds and feeds, others are more interested in the value proposition.

▶ Customer and success stories are golden. Express your company and product from the perspective of your customers and show the value you deliver.

▶ Cover your future– how will you grow and differentiate in the future?

Rebecca Lieb is an independent analyst who was formerly with Altimeter Group. Here she shows another value of briefings.

At Altimeter, there was a system for sharing tagged, cloud-based briefing notes that put all briefing information at the fingertips of all the company's analysts and researchers. That made our jobs easier when we were trying to find information on specific types of companies or businesses, and it benefits the companies we speak with, too. Vendors are made more visible to more people.

A good briefing needs great preparation. The AR manager sets everything in motion:

▶ Provide background on the analyst (bio and research)

▶ Share past engagements with your firm

▶ Set tangible goals for the briefing (change their perspective, strengthen the relationship, raise their awareness of your company, etc.)

▶ Define the briefing experience that will achieve the goals

▶ Build the briefing deck

Analysts want to know about developments within your company before the general market does. Be sure to brief them before your announcements to the marketplace. Briefings are part of the overall engagement plan that keeps you relevant and top of their minds. How often? Cadence is important. Figure that out for each analyst and put it on your calendar. Out of sight, out of mind, and you may be out of luck. Stay in touch.

Peter O'Neill talks about the relevance of briefing regularly.

> Briefings are very important. "Nothing's happening" is a dangerous scenario! If you don't have a new product release within six months or within a year, please don't stop talking to the analysts for that reason, because the analyst will start realizing they haven't heard anything from the vendor for nine months, they have gone quiet, they're not very active. At the same time, we haven't got their name mentioned in the inquiry process. That impression can get quite strong and it may be misleading. So, yeah, you don't have to have a new product to give a briefing. Keep engaging. It's important.

Deciding on Briefing topics

The briefing plan will include both company-driven topics (product announcement, shift in strategy, business updates) and analyst driving content (research agenda, relationship objectives).

Here is a simplified view of how you integrate topics with analysts to create a briefing plan. Your plan may have many more topics and probably many more analysts to brief, but the concept is the same.

	Analyst 1	Analyst 2	Analyst 3	Analyst 4	Analyst 4	Analyst 5
Big Product announcement	X	X	X		X	
Company Introduction				X		
Business Update		X			X	X

For the analysts who write research, learn their research agenda. This gives you insight into what they care about and the right opportunity and timing for engagement. Find out what relates to your company's messages and announcements. Understand their timelines so you can get them information when they are collecting it. Be the one that makes their job easier and their research better. It will build the relationship, and increase your rate of mentions and coverage as a great side benefit.

According to Rik Turner of Omdia, knowing the analyst research agenda is the key to a great relationship and a powerful engagement plan.

> The most responsive analyst teams ask you for an advance view of your research agenda. They define what is relevant to them and make sure the analyst knows their point of view on that topic. That tells them when to touch base with the analyst about particulate topics. Whereas everybody and anybody, large and small vendors, are interested in the big evaluation reports, the really great firms will engage with you on the topics you are writing about that are not product oriented. They will share their view on that market segment or emerging technology area, for example. They connect me with somebody who is researching that topic. There may not be anything concrete going on in the market, but the vendor is thinking and planning for it. That is very useful to me. If they can get those topics early, it makes for a robust series of engagements.

Pitching the briefing

The first step in a specific briefing is to determine which analysts are interested in the topic, and get agreement to do the briefing at all. Taking briefings is voluntary, and the analyst will only agree if the briefing is relevant and interesting. Therefore, consider a briefing request like a sales pitch – you must promise value to earn their attention and time. Know your prospect before you pitch.

Charlene Li, founder of Altimeter and formerly with Forrester, shares her perspective:

> Now, just because you request a briefing doesn't mean you get one! I accept briefings based on the merits of the request. The best way to get a briefing is to be right square in the middle of an analyst's current research stream. In general, I won't take a briefing unless I plan to use the information within the next three months. And there are times when I would like to get a briefing, but my calendar is full (in which case, I usually ask for information via email). So look at my current research and do a search for topics I've commented on.

> Make sure to promise me good, relevant information and make me smarter. Tell me how I will come out of it thinking differently, with your vision of how the world is changing and how your company is going to make a difference. And make it a short briefing – 30 minutes – to make it more likely that I will attend and that the call will be efficient.

Some firms require detailed information in advance of a briefing. Some vendors find this onerous and prefer not to do it. RedMonk asks for such information, and James Governor gives a good perspective on the value of providing it.

> Often in a briefing the first five to ten slides are "set up" about a company – its goals, revenues, capabilities and so on. The kind of thing that could potentially be bypassed by a set-up questionnaire that captures the key information about a firm and content of the briefing (such as company overview, market position, capabilities, vision for the future).

> Is filling out this information really such a pain for analyst relations professionals? Isn't providing information a key part of the role? I must be missing something. I have received far more intrusive questionnaires from major vendors before they deign to brief me.

> It seems to me that the purpose of a briefing is to get under the skin of a subject rather than skimming the surface. With that in mind a little prep is a good thing – why shouldn't the vendor help at this point?

> And while we're on the subject – one of AR's jobs is surely to research the analyst market, and analyst in question, and prepare an executive before

he briefs an analyst, isn't it? Research is a two-way street, a conversation, not a broadcast. With that in mind I think questionnaires are probably acceptable.

If you refuse to provide this in advance, you may well find the analyst becomes less interested in your business. Time is the analyst's most important asset, and making extra demands on their time, especially for a briefing (remember this is not a client call) is not a great basis for a smooth relationship. Should an analyst know their market already? Absolutely. But do we need to be confrontational all the time? I think not. Obviously a lot depends on context, and the degree of depth asked for in a pre-briefing questionnaire. But a blanket refusal doesn't make sense to me.

Finally there is the question of follow up, after a briefing, where the AR person has to go and find information that wasn't available during the call, which is surely quite time-consuming. Wouldn't it be better to get that out of the way first?

Spokespeople

If a briefing is theatre, the AR professional is also the casting director. It is essential to line up the right spokesperson. Deeply understand the analyst's coverage and interests and match the right person on your end. Analysts with a strategic view of the market want to hear your company's vision and strategy from executives. Analysts that dig into details want appropriate subject matter experts. Some want both. The same analyst may require a different type of spokesperson for different briefings for different purposes. Know your goals, know your analysts, engage the right one, and match the right spokesperson.

Robin Bloor gives us some strategy for identifying the right spokespeople, based on topic and analyst. He talks about product depth, which is a critical consideration. Not all analysts are looking for this, but if that's who they want, that's who we present.

Ideally, there should be three people from the vendor side doing the briefing. One is the AR person, taking notes and actions, and prodding presenters by Instant Messenger if need be – if it all starts to turn to custard. One presenter does the presenting and the other is the back-up, who steps in if needed. One should be marketing and one technical.

Just as you set a thief to catch a thief, you should send a technician to brief a technician. If you don't, you risk having a poor opinion of your product proliferate. Even on a good day, an analyst with good technical skills is capable of assuming that the deficiency is in the product, as well as the presenter.

Either analysts are trying to understand the world of technology or they are not. If they are not, then they are not really analysts, they are reporters. This is not to be despised by the way, good reporters provide a valuable service. But analysts analyze. Analysts hunger for understanding. Analysts despise marketing gloss and like technical detail. Most of all, analysts like talking to people who have a deep understanding of technology. Given the choice, any analyst worth his or her salt will want to spend time with the best technical man or woman in your company, who might be the CEO or the CTO or simply the one that runs the team that builds the most important product you sell. (Important to know the analyst to know if they want to hear high level strategy and direction from a C-level or in-depth product details. Get them the person who matches what they need.)

Jeremiah Owyang, founder of Kaleido, covered this topic back when he was a Forrester analyst. He has a different angle: rather than a technology expert, he wants to hear details of the message and positioning.

It's a real challenge for companies to identify what they are, and having a seasoned marketer on board really helps. You could risk going too high, and be filled with Marketese, Hyperbole, Mission Statements, and bunch of buzzwords; or too low, and focus on technology alone, without providing business context. For many startups, they are a bunch of technologists that may not have business skills. It's time to invest in someone who understands communication, presentation, marketing, business development and the marketplace.

For Ray Wang, the spokesperson who can give the details of the subject is the one he wants. As always, the focus of the briefing determines the expert you choose.

I want to talk to a marketing guy that actually has influenced the market, a product strategy woman who can actually show me the specifics and talk about the future, a customer service and delivery person who can show me what it's really like working with your company, an executive who can really get stuff done. I want a real conversation.

The pre-briefing

The pre-briefing is a fabulous thing - a rare practice that should be done more often by more AR folks. It not only helps us to prepare a better briefing, it helps to avoid an utter and total disaster. The pre-briefing helps ensure the main round hits all marks.

Robin Bloor gives us good insights on the value of pre-briefing.

> A common scenario is that a technology company is launching a new product and it decides to hold a series of press and analyst briefings.
>
> It is advisable to pre-brief one analyst before you talk to any others or any journalists. You may believe that you've got the marketing and technology message right, but if you haven't you'll probably be given a bad time by the analysts and also by the press (many of whom talk to analysts). You need to test your marketing message and for that reason you need a "friendly analyst" to help.
>
> If you are a large company, you know this and you'll have paid an analyst or two to do some message testing before you face the music and dance. But if you're small you will not have the money. So you need a friendly analyst who understands your technology area.
>
> Why would a "friendly analyst" help you for nothing?
>
> Actually they won't. They will expect that if they give you some free consultancy, you will realize you owe them and hire them at a later date to do: white-paper work, surveys, presentations, webinars, podcast, direct consultancy et al. There's no free lunch here, it's an informal trade. You're selling to them and they're selling to you, but no money changes hands.
>
> Some analyst companies (or individuals) will never help unless they see the dollars first, but some will. You would be ill advised to try to just exploit an analyst who is helpful. Analysts talk to each other and are powerful influencers, both for and against. They have long memories too.
>
> So, if you have a limited budget, it makes sense to cultivate a long term relationship with one or two analysts for that reason.
>
> How Do You Conduct The Pre-Briefing?

The pre-briefing is a rehearsal. On the one hand you "follow the script" and on the other you interact with the analyst taking note of whatever he or she says. You may even want to record the briefing. There are some obvious things you want the analyst to verify:

- ❷ Did the technology message make sense and was it easily understood?
- ❷ Did the business benefits explanation make sense?
- ❷ Does it need a demo?
- ❷ Was there anything goofy about the presentation?

My advice is to have a check-list and use it.

What Happens If You Do Not Do a Pre-Briefing?

Your team may be so good that it usually gets it right. However, the penalty for getting it wrong is high. You never get a second chance to make a first impression. With a product launch you are in first impression territory. Some vendors' presentations get savaged. I've savaged one or two myself. If an analyst thinks you're wasting his/her time, they will be annoyed and you will have wasted your own time too. Also your message will have been completely lost.

Briefing dos and don'ts

There are many perspectives on what makes a good briefing. We present a number of opinions below. Some common themes are evident:

- ▸ Target the briefing to the analyst's interest
- ▸ Don't waste time on generic industry background
- ▸ Be open and honest
- ▸ Have the right spokespeople on the call
- ▸ Cover the business benefits, not just technology specifics.

Josh Zelonis wrote this back when he was a Forrester analyst.

I'm an analyst. It's my job to formulate opinions on your product and company and provide that insight to my clients. Prior to joining Forrester, the impact analysts have on the industry was described to me this way: "I don't have time to be an expert at everything I need to know, so I engage analyst firms to provide me that expertise." Most of the time, clients are looking for a very short list of vendors. Here's how to get on that list:

Use visual aids, and have a game plan. Nobody likes death by PowerPoint, but if you schedule time on my calendar, then show up to a briefing with no slides and expect me to ask you questions, I'm going to interpret this as you not valuing my time. Take it a step farther, and email me the slides after the call because I frequently refer back to these when I need a quick refresher on your company, and it's a good way to get your contact info into my address book if I have any questions.

Start off by telling me what you're selling. I believe in the elevator pitch. If you can't get me interested in a couple of sentences, then you either don't understand what you're selling, or you aren't confident that you're filling a need. You wouldn't believe how many companies get multiple slides into a deck, talking about everything from founder experience to how great their venture capital backing is, and then start describing a problem I'm probably already familiar with while I'm left to solve the problem myself since I still haven't been told what they're selling yet. This leads me to the next point…

Assume I already understand the problem and have probably written about it. I don't need you to go all Dostoyevsky with the problem statement, and your customers probably don't need that either. If they do, they don't have the problem and aren't a prospect. See what I did there? Acknowledge the problem, so I know you understand my client's needs, and move on to how you are uniquely solving the problem.

Help me understand your vision for the way things should be. What is the offering, and how is it deployed? What other requirements am I committing to with this product? Show me the "Marketecture Diagram," so I can start to understand what the product does and how it integrates into other solutions. I've also heard this called the "CTO Slide." This is also your opportunity to talk about roadmaps because you're never going to be done improving your product, and this will help me understand what you're striving to become.

And this from Anton Chuvakin, former Gartner analyst.

DO NOT:

- Do not bring a 110 slide deck and then fly through it. Analysts will not retain the information.

- Do not spend time talking about your team — in fact, don't tell me anything I can read on your "About Us" page [we are analysts, NOT investors, a brief "who we are" slide is OK].

- Do not go so fast that an analyst cannot ask questions, but also do not stop every three minutes to ask whether an analyst has any questions.

- Do not be vague about what your product/service actually does in real life [this, as you can easily guess, is a biggie!]

- Do not focus excessively on marketing and "the story you tell" at a cost of product functionality, specific problems you solve and precise reasons why your approach is superior to alternatives.

- Do not spend too much time [or: any time] on industry statistics about how bad the threat is. We see this every time. Do focus on explaining the specific problem your product/service tackles.

- Do not allude to having many customers and then say "but they are so secretive we cannot share anything about them."

- Do not assign somebody who is unqualified, disorganized and arrogant to the task of doing a vendor briefing.

- Similarly, do not bring "a CTO" who cannot answer technical questions; because if your CTO is fake, perhaps your entire product is?

- Do not lie to an analyst such as by saying that you are fascinated by their brilliant research while it becomes clear you actually never read it.

- Do not ask for a briefing under NDA, unless you have some really, really, really good reasons for it (this is very rare!)

- Do not focus on bashing your competition [such as with rumors and innuendo], but do provide a crisp, fact-based comparison to the competition you fight in the field.

DO:

- ● Do bring a well-organized slide deck that you actually plan to follow (please no "let's skip to slide 48"). Some analysts recommend 10–20 slides, which I think is a bit more is acceptable, as long as they tell a coherent story.

- ● You should make sure you tell the problem you solve and what makes you different in the first 10 minutes of the briefing. Be sure to describe this as a unique value for end users, not a unique marketing story.

- ● Do express your views on the market history, evolution, trends and your role in all this — but do not give us the market basics.

- ● Ideally, share why we need yet another vendor, in this market, to do this [if you are a player in a very competitive market]. A free tip: if you cannot explain this to an analyst, you definitely will not explain it to a prospect....

- ● If you are going to focus on your product strategy, please understand what the word means: a real strategy defines the actions you are taking to grow, help clients and beat the competition.

- ● Do provide a fact-based slide comparing your approach to alternatives, direct competitors or even the old way of solving the same problem.

- ● Do remember what you presented to this analyst in the past [we don't like an introductory briefing two months after your introductory briefing...]

- ● If an analyst asks a question, please answer concisely, and take no more than 30–60 seconds doing so.

- ● Do cover the exact problems you solve, broad product architecture, top competitors you see (and, please don't say THERE ARE NONE!), customer use cases, your largest deployments, roadmap [that you plan to actually follow!], etc.

- ● Some of us care about your pricing and your pricing strategy, but some [typically us GTP analysts] don't. Ask an analyst whether they want to know your pricing mechanics.

- ● Most of us care at least somewhat about your number of production customers and/or revenue. Please share at least something on this even if you are very secretive.

- If you want to really impress, perhaps even shed some light on what lessons you learned selling, deploying and helping customers operate your product.

Wendy Nather shared these insights.

Briefing an analyst is different from selling to a customer. Don't use the same deck. The Jedi sales mind tricks won't work, and will just be annoying.

Remember, an analyst has maybe half an hour (or an hour if you're lucky) to figure out and understand something you may have been working on for months or years. Ask how THEY want to learn it (maybe it's not PowerPoint). I myself prefer to use a hands-on demo.

451 alum Fernando Montenegro exemplifies this; "When taking a briefing, I tell a vendor to speak to me as if I'm two people: as a VC interested in your business and as a technical buyer interested in your product. Answers in both domains should be comprehensive."

▸ Don't waste time setting up the problem. The analyst already knows what the problem/threat/risk/concept is. Go straight to how you address it.

▸ Don't assume the analyst isn't technical; let her have as many details as she wants.

▸ Because time is so short, the analyst can't spend time proving or refuting your claims; she can only report them. It's no use pointing out that your competitor is lying unless you can prove it unequivocally. Otherwise you're just in "yuh-huh!" "nuh-uh!" territory.

▸ Don't say you're the "first" or "only" company to do something. That just made me want to prove you wrong, and 9 times out of 10, I could do it. In fact, get rid of adjectives and adverbs altogether. Just give facts. I'll make the judgment as to whether it's fast or unique.

  - Nick Patience, a co-founder of 451, reminded us of his early rule that, if you are the only one in a category, it's not a category.

▸ Just because the analyst has a different opinion doesn't mean she doesn't "get it." Don't threaten to keep briefing her until she sees it your way. Make sure she has the facts, then step back and let her analyze them.

● George Hamilton, also a recovering analyst, adds to this: One more thing: don't be defensive. If you're briefing for validation you're doing it wrong. Welcome the criticism and the holes they poke in your story. Learn and work to be better.

From Charlene Li.

▶ I have little time and little patience for what I call "background". You can assume that I'm pretty up to speed on the space!

▶ My pet peeve: companies that show up at briefings and start by saying, "So, what do you want to know?"

▶ Key information for analysts

  ● What problem are you solving?

  ● How do you create value for the user?

  ● How do you make money?

  ● How do you differentiate yourself from the competition?

  ● How will you market your product/service?

  ● What is your vision of how the market will develop, and how will you fit into it?

From Jeremiah Owyang.

▶ Understand the analysts' coverage area. Analysts get briefed by vendors very frequently, I get briefed a couple of times a week, (yesterday I had three). It's important for the analyst to know the vendors in their space, what they are working on, what's coming, and what challenges the industry is having.

▶ You need to stand out in the marketplace. It's very, very challenging. Why should you care? Because the marketplace is so large and varied, you really need to stand out in the eyes of the analyst.

▶ What a great briefing looks like. It's rare that a vendor can deliver a succinct, resonating presentation in under an hour, and I think this is a good model for others to follow:

  ● In one of the best briefings I've had, a vendor was very professional in their communication, messaging, presentation and demo. She started off with a clear message on what the company does, quickly differentiated how her company was different than the other 60, showed how her products and service brought value to customers (with little marketese or hyperbole) showed the major product suites, gave a case study starting with objectives, challenges and measurable results, summarized then passed to the demo. The product manager then showed me a live demo, cruised some of the major features, and showed a live use case, rather than just poking around at the interface. They were forthcoming as I asked where they think customers feel they need improvement.

Mike Guay covers NDA considerations.

By default, information discussed between analysts vendors and clients is under NDA. The exception to this is vendor briefings. Vendor briefings are an important source of information for analysts. Since it can sometimes be difficult to get a lot of analysts' calendar time, vendors will try to pack everything they can into a one-hour briefing.

A recommendation would be to pick three or four topics maximum to cover in the briefing. I often asked vendors "What are the two or three things you think a Gartner customer should know you about you and/ or your products?" Keep in mind that analysts interact with dozens of vendors. It's good to know what you as the vendor think is important to convey. Leave more detailed information in a deck for the analysts to review later. Analysts will reach out to AR representatives if they have questions or would like clarification on a specific topic.

Sometimes vendors will want to communicate something under non-disclosure. In those cases – and most vendors are very good at this – it is important to specifically state the topic(s) and specific, reasonable, timeframe for non-disclosure. A frequent example is letting analysts know of important information 24–48 hours in advance of a press release. This is common.

Vendors will also sometimes want to brief analysts on information such as new products or markets that may not materialize for a month or two. It is important to keep in mind that once a certain time period has passed – say 60 days – the information provided during the briefing may no longer be accurate of even relevant. If possible, keep those incidents to a minimum.

Rik Turner on overall treatment:

> I like it when the person who sets up the conversation gets out of the way and doesn't try to manage the conversation. I don't want them dipping in and out with the "official" message. I understand that they think they're doing a good job, and probably in some ways they are, but I do prefer to get the unvarnished version. We're looking for what's really going on. It behooves us to create a relationship with the spokesperson so they will trust us and tell us what's really going on. They can tell us if it's under NDA and I will respect that. When they know you will respect it, then they should be prepared to really talk to you.

Laurie McCabe talks about the value of the vendor's view of their competitors:

> It's always interesting to find out how vendors see their competitors. I do not necessarily expect a detailed analysis from them, but I do want to know where they see the biggest threats are and which competitors they come up against most, and how they are differentiating themselves. You would be amazed at how many vendors fail to really answer this question. I want to understand this so that I can compare their view of how they fit into the competitive landscape with how I view it in the context of discussions with many vendors in their space. It shows that they're not drinking too much of their own Kool-Aid and trust our relationship enough to discuss it with me. And I can share my perceptions and why they may differ with them.

Rebecca Lieb with a plea:

> Listen to us. We analysts make our living as strategic, research-based advisors. We're very well connected and ahead-of-the-curve informed about the industry sectors we microscopically cover. A briefing is hardly an advisory session, but we may well make an observation or remark that could serve you well. Listen for those nuggets.

Case studies are an important part of analyst briefings. Supply them regularly. Jeremiah Owyang gives us some best practices.

> First of all, think of a case study as telling a story: start with a start, end with the end, there is a plot, characters, opposition and an ending with a resolution. Use diagrams or slides or screenshots to supplement the discussion.

1) Define the Objective.

Define what the problem or challenge that your client was trying to overcome, express why the marketing campaign was needed in the first place. Examples of an objective could be: the need to connect with a certain audience/market, raise awareness for a product, glean insight into an existing market, or directly impact sales. Ideally the less objectives you have, the more focused your campaign will be, so try to be succinct.

2) Tell what you actually did.

In detail, outline the steps that you did for your client, include the features, services, and deployment.. Of course, each activity should align with your objective(s).

3) Define how you overcame challenges.

Many vendors are afraid to show their weaknesses, instead be forthcoming. Talk about challenges and how you overcame them or what you learned. Demonstrate your flexibility and ability to be a quick savvy marketer.

4) Tell what the costs were.

In some cases (such as an analyst briefing) it can be to your advantage to discuss costs and pricing, because: 1) The analyst can guide clients to the appropriate vendor if they have price considerations 2) The analyst likely has pricing of your marketplace and if you ask, they may tell you how you compare to market pricing (of course, never giving away confidential information). This can be on or off the record, and they will respect your wishes. Still uncomfortable? Use ranges of prices or price bands.

5) Measurable results.

This is the clincher. Provide detailed analysis and results on what you accomplished. Use numbers. For example: 100,000 new registered users were gained and 30% of them were very active resulting in an average duration of 20 minutes where 1500 of them talked about the campaign, clicked through to a microsite, or interacted with a game, etc.

Analyst Relations, like all relations, can be fraught with conflict. Analysts sit through lots of terrible briefings. Don't add to their misery. In addition to best practices, let's cover some worst practices so you know what to avoid. Owyang gives us a rundown.

My job as an industry analyst is to listen to pitches from different vendors, from small startups, to the web giants. I get paid (yes I'm a professional BS filter) to listen to their pitches – and then translate it into reality for reports and for our clients, the buyers.

Here's a few things I've learned to translate, and I'm going to share with you here now – so you, as a buyer, will know the danger zones when you're buying from a vendor. In most cases, you can skip the first five slides of any presentation, a great time to fiddle with email, smack talk on Twitter, use your iPhone, start a game of bullshit bingo, or figure out a way to sound relevant.

❖ The Famous Two-by-Two Grid

For some reason, vendors think anything in a chart is believable, even if they made it up themselves! Typically, in the first five slides of a presentation, there's a two-by-two grid where the vendor always positions in the top right. The competitors are scattered in all the other quadrants, but are never more further 'up and to the right' than the vendor. The funny thing is, the X and Y axis are often criteria that you won't find on any research report – and every vendor's two-by-two is different so they're 'up and to the right'.

Translation: *We know up and to the right is best, so we created our own X and Y axis labels, we're hoping you won't read the small print "tallest CEO" or "best ping pong players in support."*

❖ We're the "Industry Leader."

I've heard this one over and over, in fact everyone's an industry leader at something. "Industry leader in Facebook on Tuesdays" or "Industry leader in community interactions in Fresno at YMCA." The trick here is to ask them who determined they were the industry leader, and if the category is large – and believable enough.

Translation: *Leading is a good term to use, but the size of the industry and how we segment is up to us, don't ask questions as we'll just tell you "We'll get back to you on those details."*

✓ The Logo Smorgasbord

Vendors love to put many logos on one of the first 10 slides, it's meant to amaze you and show that they are with it with the big brands. The trick here is that even the smallest of deployments will validate a logo on that slide – and sometimes without the permission of that brand. If you're interviewing competitors you'll notice that many of them share the same customers as others in their space, it's likely true. I often see Cisco, IBM, Microsoft, and other big tech companies on nearly every logo slide from even competitors.

Translation: *The more logos we cram on here the more you'll be impressed, if you rotate your head back and forth real fast, it's kinda like a kaleidoscope... but digital.*

✓ The Fallacy of Vendor Math

You've probably heard vendor math before: "We've 39 of the Fortune 50" or a variation on a theme "17 of the top 20 pharmaceutical companies use us", or we've 150% year on year in new clients in enterprise space. While factual, deciding on numerators and denominators can be tweaked to fit the needs of every vendor. Secondly, the universe of "Fortune" companies changes annually, if not more frequently. Vendor math may sound impressive – but it's likely skewed, of course, this is coming from the 7th most popular Jeremiah in most Google searches.

Translation: *Whoever told you numbers never lie was right, 'cept perspective is a son of a gun. We didn't want to tell you that 150% year on year growth of new enterprise clients could be going from two customers to five (but one was my brother's company).*

✓ Our Many Awards

Everyone loves a shiny trophy, and we see accolades and awards from just about every vendor. Contests from blogs, conferences, editors, and even analysts. With everyone getting awards, and touting it too, it's hard to put any real value on any of them.

Translation: *We hope you're impressed with this shout out and award from this blogspot blogger three years ago–it's hanging next to our elk head in the den by the wetbar.*

Now if you're a vendor (or perhaps their PR agency), don't be offended. Use this information to improve your communications. In all due fairness, if someone has a list of 'translating Analyst/Client speak' I'll link to it here too.

Briefing Outcomes

Great briefings are great. Everyone high fives and hurrays. Other briefings are not that great. Track the outcomes of your briefings so you can learn, improve, and follow up with individual analysts. This will help you plan the next steps that will help in every relationship.

Here Robin Bloor lays out some less than optimum outcomes.

The primary goal of every analyst briefing is to communicate the corporate message (about a product, service or whatever) accurately. If that didn't happen in the briefing, then it failed. But some briefings will fail, because:

1. The analyst "didn't get it" (it happens quite frequently).
2. The analyst got it, but disagrees that your product/service is worthwhile.
3. The analyst was in "one of those moods."
4. The presentation went off track.

If the outcome is **1.** your company's marketing message is poor or the presentation is poor or the presenter was poor. Some corrective action is necessary. It's too late for this briefing, but the next one may be okay.

If the outcome is **2.** you are in trouble. It could be the marketing message, or presentation or presenter, but most likely there's better technology out there – or at least the analyst thinks there is. It is imperative to find out why.

If the outcome appears to be **3.** you're probably dealing with a difficult analyst whose bonnet is inhabited by a bee. Take a note and move on. If all analysts you brief behave this way, then this is not a case of 3. it's 1. or 2. I talked to an AR professional who said that for one product launch, virtually every analyst was critical (or worse) of the product. It was awful, but there was the consolation that none of the analysts came from the same company, so none of them knew that all the other analysts had reacted negatively.

If the outcome is **4.** – you ran out of time because the analyst decided to spend 45 minutes discussing the recent success of his favorite soccer team, or something like that – it's your fault. The AR person should step in and control the briefing if it starts to veer off course.

The Other Outcome: Useful Input

Most of what analysts say will be useful input. If they're like me they will probe technical angles, marketing terminology, sales objections, business benefits, your knowledge of your competitors and so on. It's useful if what they say is unique and it's useful if they repeat what everyone else said. It's all useful. That means you have to take notes and you must collate the notes once the briefing series is over.

The briefing is our basic engagement with the analyst community, and almost always the first step. It is an important way we make them aware of our company and keep them informed on important developments. It helps keep us top of mind and relevant. Do them right. Briefings are essential steps on the path to great and productive relationships.

But briefings alone can only take you so far. They lack feedback. They lack real dialogue and interaction. In order to build a relationship, it is necessary to engage in more depth and spend more time.

Chapter Six

Inquiries, Strategy Days and Events

*F*acts are not enough. You are off to a great start when an analyst knows your strategy, message, and products, but let's not forget the "R" in AR. Our job is to build a relationship between the analyst, our company, and ourselves. The human connection is critical to our work. When the analyst knows the people and culture that form your company, their perception becomes clearer, fuller, and more connected. Understanding builds trust. Trust builds the bond that enables you to change attitudes and make a difference for your company.

Inquiries

A good AR program knows how to run a great inquiry, and does it often. Great inquiries give your company feedback, insight, advice and recommendations. They also build great relationships by changing the nature of the interaction between the company and the analyst. Think of it as the analyst sitting on your side of the table, talking through problems, expounding on their wisdom, bonding with you. Contrast that with a briefing where you're sitting on the far side of the table pitching, where they are listening passively, where you sound like every other vendor, and where the analyst starts to yawn. Nobody yawns at their own opinion. That is the magic of inquiries.

A great inquiry gives all parties nuggets of insight. You get insights you can take action on. The analyst gets feedback from you in an open forum. Best of all, it strengthens your relationships with the analysts that matter.

Inquiries are free and usually unlimited with the firms you have a commercial relationship with. Analysts are required to take inquiries and usually are credited in some way for them. They are an often underutilized arrow in your quiver. Use them.

Keep these basics in mind to bring the most value to your inquiries:

▸ Prepare thoroughly with good questions that dig into the focus of the inquiry. Put questions in priority order so the most important questions will get covered. A great inquiry is like a great conversation – it will run off on its own in any direction and find depth where you didn't anticipate. Make sure the topics you need to be covered are covered, in case you and the analyst get hyper-engaged, just like you hoped.

▸ Share smartly. Use your topics and questions to demonstrate your intelligent understanding of the market.

▸ Listen carefully.

▸ Apply the insights. Make sure to identify what is actionable, and drive that action through the organization. Make your inquiries a source of expert knowledge and a window into the competitive marketplace. Do that well, and you mark your AR program as a source of extremely high strategic value.

Peter O'Neill, a former Forrester analyst and now an independent, gives us an analyst view of the value of inquiry.

A Forrester analyst does about 50 inquiries per quarter. About 80% are end users (buyers), 15% are vendors and about 5% are financial analysts, venture capital companies, and press people. I generally want to take inquiries because they are a great way to find information for my research. I hear what the client says to me about problems they are facing in their project, what vendors they are mentioning but also – of course – what vendors they don't mention. Although clients pay me to talk to them, I collect a lot of information through the inquiries.

The most interesting, productive vendor interactions I have had are with those that are really interested in what I say to them. That is rewarding, because sometimes at the end of the year when they announce something I say "I was part of that! I suggested that! That's my word!" That of course makes you think totally differently about what they're announcing.

On the other hand, there are vendors who I disagree with entirely. They turn around and blame AR for the analyst not being briefed properly. They don't take in information and advice, they see the relationship as only one way.

Mike Guay covers some best practices in using inquiry:

Preparation is everything. The best scenario is where the vendor comes with well thought out issues or topics. Sometimes vendors will be direct and request feedback on a statement – such as "we think [pick a topic] – what do you think?" or "Are you hearing this from the customers you speak to?"

Generic questions such as "what are you hearing from your customers?" may not be relevant to what the vendor wants to know and does not take the best advantage of an analyst's advice and knowledge. Many topics are very nuanced and it takes a good analyst to understand what's going on with the players, what the customers are looking for, what the trends are, etc.

The vendor might already have a position or perception in mind, but ask the analyst what they think. If the analyst is aligned with their thinking, great – that can provide reinforcement. If not, why not? Vendors want to understand analyst thinking in detail and discuss how they see the topic. They understand that analysts can have a broader perspective on the market just by virtue of what they do. Analysts often have years of experience in an industry, and speak to a wide variety of decision makers at customers like C-suite executives and functional area leads such as CFOs, COOs, VPs of HR, etc. That perspective provides a lot of added value, but is more relevant when focused on a specific topic.

An example of this might be – "We are considering adding [functionality] to our core product. Do you hear customers asking for this, or are they more likely to see a focused solution from a third party provider?"

James Governor reiterates:

The conversational nature of an inquiry, where the analyst doesn't hold back on any advice, can be a great learning experience for both parties, cementing understanding of a product or service and its positioning in the minds of both the client and the analyst.

Mark Smith points out how one-way communications fail to take advantage of what an analyst can really offer.

> Using analysts to get input and feedback to help optimize activities going on is sometimes at odds with what AR teams must do. Because vendors are usually behind internally, the AR team is in a position to present something to the analyst that might only be a week or two before launch and it's basically 95% baked. I always ask – do you want feedback that can impact this stuff, because I don't want to spend cycles giving a bunch of feedback that's not going to be used. That's not effective. I see more of that with the pandemic as there seems to be more scrambling around trying to get things out, and less strategic activity. AR is at the mercy of the CEO, head of marketing, and product marketing whether they can be strategic. They're just trying to get stuff out.

Strategy Days

Strategy days provide a full session with an important analyst. They are a major endeavor that AR pros need to manage. Understanding the perspective of the analyst helps make them strong and effective.

Ray Wang draws on a lot of experience from both sides of a strategy day:

> I learned a lot about strategy days when I was on the vendors side doing product management and product marketing for software companies.

> As an AR pro planning a strategy day, you have to put yourself into that mindset. What is the company looking for, what do you want to get out of the analyst? Competitive intelligence? Feedback on what customers are looking for? Marketing message? Ideas or suggestions around a problem you want to solve?

> After getting clear on the purpose, the quality and level of your advisory day will really be dictated by the quality and level of the analyst. There are several scenarios:

> Scenario one is brand new analysts that may have come from a competitor. Scenario two is a little bit different: You're in the middle of an evaluation and you have no choice, you got a gun to your head. Scenario three – and that's the fun one – is when you have an analyst that understands your space and you truly want to learn from them.

If someone's new to a space and you're trying to get them trained, the idea of the strategy day is really about helping them get more informed about the company, build relationships, help them understand the product direction, especially if the analyst came from a competitor, from industry, and you really want them to see how it really works in your company.

In the second scenario, with an analyst that does an evaluation report, you need to make sure they come away with the best impression possible of your company. You consider this an important part of the yearly evaluation cycle. Sometimes you're dealing with an analyst who hasn't done their job and you're trying to fill in. Other times your objective is just to get their interest, and this is totally dependent on the analyst. Sometimes the only way to get their attention is to do things that are a bit extraordinary. It could be a great customer engagement, it could be an experience they never had before. One time, when I was with a vendor, we took an influential analyst to Israel to meet with a bunch of start-ups because he had this thing for start-ups in Israel. Really? But fine. It worked. Part of the game.

The third scenario – the fun one – is different. You have back and forth interaction and the ideas flow. They tell you the trends they're seeing in the market, and you talk about your view. The vendor talks about what they're rolling out and you give them real feedback. We discuss who they're targeting and what they want. We can have great discussions, but it's hard to do that if you don't have the trust and you don't have an analyst that actually knows your space and talks to buy side clients.

In Richard Stiennon's view, strategy sessions can lead to some interesting conclusions on the part of the analyst.

Gartner and many other firms will hire out their analysts for daylong strategy sessions. The most fun and productive are the rare occasions when this is for an end user client. Most of the time, these Strategic Advisory Services (SAS) days are with vendors. The analyst flies out, stays in a hotel, drives to the vendor site, and spends a day getting completely briefed on the vendor's products, services, sales strategy, marketing plans, and future developments.

The vendor gets value out of the time spent, first by hopefully influencing the analyst to think positively about them, and second from the strategic advice the analyst gives. Gartner used to pay the analyst a bonus of a couple hundred dollars for each day (for which they charged the vendor $12,000), but today there are no financial benefits to the analyst for SAS days. I used to do 50 SAS days a year. That is one of the things that got me thinking about being on my own. 50 x $12k = $600k! Not bad work if you can get it. The fee today for an analyst day is closer to $25,000.

Events

Live analyst events may be a relic of old. In the COVID-19 world, everything is virtual, but someday, life may get back to normal. If and when it does, this advice is very relevant.

Whether held in conjunction with a vendor user event or as a stand-alone gathering, analyst events are a great opportunity to impress all of your important analysts at once. Done well, these events are memorable and give high value. Every vendor does them, so you want to stand out. But never let "pizzazz" get in the way of an event's purpose. Meet analysts' needs and expectations at every step.

John Sumser of HRExaminer attends many of these events, and sees mutual value for the analyst and vendor.

> You should understand these analyst confabs. Held in an interesting hotel, they are day-long gabfests where the conversation is led by key executives. The analysts get an opportunity to hear the company's story; the company gets an opportunity to tell it. In a perfect world, the company would know each analyst well enough to deliver the appropriate slice of the picture. In the real world, companies use these get-togethers as a test ground for their market pitches. The analysts are a somewhat harsh audience, so new spin gets a good going over.

James Governor pushes the idea of simple considerations for the analyst.

1. Have customers, partners and technologists at the event; encourage them to talk to the analysts in informal settings.
2. Don't try and cram so much into the day that analysts have no time to catch up with other work items.
3. Make sure free Wi-Fi is available (see 2).
4. Have the event close to most of your target analysts, rather than in an exotic location (greener and more convenient).

5. Keep presentations short and to the point.
6. Have plenty of breaks, otherwise known as water-cooler moments (see 2).
7. Tell stories and have no more than about three key narratives you want the analysts to leave with.

He also give us some best practices for AR's role in these events.

A great event I attended was just customer presentations. That was it. The customers were happy to talk about what they were doing.

AR didn't play a support role, it was very much their gig. There was a lovely moment when a company sales rep evidently tasked with "vertical go-to-market solutions" or something – leaned over and asked one of the customers – how do we find you/what are you doing here? The answer – a swift nod to AR "He asked us".

What I am saying is that AR is building relations with customers and ISVs, not just the analyst community. AR is being active in engaging with customers, without waiting for corporate to bring content on a plate. One implication of that is in some cases, the reference may say something that makes the corporation squirm just a little bit – but that is as it should be.

This was an event where real work got done. The product may be a work in progress, but the natural assets are very healthy, notably in terms of customer relationships.

James' peer at RedMonk, Stephen O'Grady, adds his view on lower ambitions for an event's content as a way to be more effective.

As many AR folks know, I'm not an early riser, and don't enjoy breakfast events in any context – irrespective of how much socializing was done the night before. When I suggested to an event organizer at one point a while back that I was not alone in my distaste for the often absurdly early start times, they responded, "so, what, we go later?" My response was, "no, just do less." Sadly, that's not an option for many AR event organizers.

To be sure, I understand the organizer's dilemma; they're pressed from all sides by people intent on getting a piece of the action, so to speak, at what might be the only face-to-face event they'll have with the analysts that year. But if you can look at it from the perspective of an attendee, this shouldn't be our problem. Attentive and interested as we may all be, the human attention span is what it is. I try not to schedule anything – consults, events, interviews, whatever – for slots greater than 90 minutes. Against that backdrop, sessions beginning at the crack of dawn and concluding with late dinners are not likely to yield the results you might expect them to. Because attention wanders, inevitably.

And if the expectation is not – as I've been told occasionally – that the folks at the conference will be enraptured from the early morning till the early evening, why schedule the event that way? The best conferences that I attend are those with flexible agendas that allow for conversation, discourse and dialogue. Death by PowerPoint and briefing is available to us more or less any time we want; the opportunity to interact face to face with your employees is not. But conference schedules tend to optimize for the former, at the expense of the latter.

Ultimately, this isn't really about the start time: it's about realizing that conferences should be about the attendees at least as much – if not more so – than the event organizers. While it may seem counterintuitive that messaging us less will allow us to absorb more, it's been more or less universally true in my experience.

Henry Morris, formerly of IDC, shares a common view held among analysts prior to COVID.

When scheduling analyst events skip the fancy, but inconveniently located resorts. Most analysts travel so much that they are no longer impressed by fancy resorts. What they appreciate are vendors that are considerate of their time and energy by making events convenient. Select event locations close to airports and consider flight timing when setting the agenda.

Meetings with executives

Your top executives are critical players in your AR strategy as they represent the overall company. They lend prestige to a presentation. They let the analyst know not only how important the message and the meeting is, but also how important the analyst is. Your C-levels are capital. Spend them well. Analysts want to know them, and top firms expect to know them.

If you are trying to build a relationship between your company and a top tier analyst, think about how you can cultivate the connection. Consider a "buddy system" where each Tier 1 analyst is matched with an appropriate executive who develops and maintains a more casual relationship. In addition to the formal briefings and other engagements, they should touch base regularly – meet for a drink when in town together, exchange quick emails, have an occasional chat. People like people. People are influenced by people.

You are a source of wisdom about analysts to these executives. They don't know the analysts and the AR process like you do. Advise them how to fit into the strategy that you designed.

Mark Smith shares how the executive perspective offers a great view to complement what an analyst hears on the ground, and the value the analyst can deliver when positioned at this level.

> When an analyst meets with an executive of a company, it's a different level of conversation than with the product manager types we usually meet with. There's an exchange on point of view on the market the company is focused on. The analyst is trying to understand what elements of the company strategy are being executed in the market. Is it around particular product lines? Is it about partnerships? Is it around the direct or indirect parts of the business? It depends on the specific executive. The executive is trying to get a perspective on the marketplace, because a lot of times they're not getting an unvarnished point of view from inside the organization. They are trying to get inputs from across the market on things that may have surfaced internally.

Bob Parker, lead analyst at IDC, works specifically with executives at some of the largest firms in the world. He notes the value an analyst firm can bring when they are privy to the executive view of a company.

> I use executive conversations to understand the strategic thinking of an organization and communicate their priorities to the individual analysts on my team. This gives the analysts an overall view of the company, which is great context for conversations at the product manager level. That helps the executives, too. We're a third party reinforcing their strategy messages.
>
> At large organizations the agendas can be out of sync. The product manager focuses on delivering what the customer is asking for to sell the product today. They get kudos based on the revenue that the product generates, not on how well they support the strategy. The strategy and

product manager are out of sync. The executive conversations we have bring that into the light.

Inquiries, strategy sessions and events are an important part of any AR program. They give you a variety of ways to engage with different objectives. Applying the right techniques to the right analysts helps meet your goals.

Chapter Seven:

Evaluation Reports

*L*et the shudders begin.

When analyst firms kick off reports like the Gartner Magic Quadrant, the Forrester Wave, or the IDC Marketscape, hard work begins. Vendors respond with hours of work on surveys, briefings, demos and customer references. These reports are important, and achieving a great position is grabbing the brass ring. They are visible internally and externally and can make a significant difference in a vendor's top line.

For many executives, these reports are all that AR is about. You know better. Educate them. Great placement is just the tip of an iceberg that represents an enormous amount of year-round effort and expertise.

Though much has been written about evaluation reports from the perspective of vendors, here is a rare glimpse of the analyst side.

Richard Stiennon talks about the process at Gartner with the MQ.

> Here is how Magic Quadrants are created, based on my four years as the primary author of two Magic Quadrants and secondary author on several more. It is also derived from my knowledge of changes to the process since I left. Thanks to frequent challenges to their process and objectivity from disgruntled vendors, Gartner has put a lot of work into improving their methodology. I also work with many vendors on their responses to the surveys Gartner sends out for Magic Quadrants, so I have seen this evolution first hand.

> Each Magic Quadrant has at least one primary author and possibly several secondary authors, depending on the size and importance of a product category. The responsibility for creating an MQ is the most onerous task a Gartner Analyst has. (Creating 18-slide PowerPoint presentations for Summits and Symposia is the next most onerous task.)

Analysts dread the process. They like to be thinking about and researching the next big thing, not re-hashing ground they covered over and over.

In most cases, the MQ for a particular category already exists. The analyst either was present at the inception or inherited the MQ from another analyst who has moved up, moved on to other areas of coverage, or left Gartner altogether.

The publication of MQs used to be scheduled to coincide with the Gartner IT Symposium at Disney World every fall, but today that is not adhered to as strictly. Their presentations are supposed to include updated Magic Quadrants for their sectors. Often the official schedule for MQs is for a new one to appear every six months. Because of the tremendous workload, this often gets collapsed into one every twelve months, which is actually a blessing for the vendors. Responding to the MQ surveys is an arduous task, too.

First the analyst must decide who makes the cut for the next version of the MQ. They look at all the vendors who have been acquired or, thanks to their inside knowledge, are about to be acquired. They determine what the inclusion criteria will be, often a gross revenue measure but sometimes a new requirement based on changes to the market. Throughout the year they would have been making notes about new vendors to include, usually as niche vendors, based on the 200-400 vendor briefings they have participated in.

The analyst then refines the spreadsheet containing the 20-150 questions that are going to be used to generate the positions in the Magic Quadrant. In addition to the actual questions, they come up with the secret weightings that are applied to each answer from each vendor. The questionnaires are usually broken down into business questions and product capability questions that line up with the Ability to Execute and Completeness of Vision axes.

The analyst must then send the questionnaire to the contact person on record at each vendor. This is the part they dread. It is the official kick-off of the vendor response cycle. Savvy vendors use this phase to schedule briefings and inquiries (if they are clients) to get clarification on what the analyst is thinking. It could mean fifteen or more scheduled calls for the analyst, all to discuss the upcoming MQ.

When the vendors respond by the required time, with the usual pleas for extensions, the responses are reviewed and combined into one spreadsheet. A score, or rating, is given to each answer, and each question has a weight associated with it: low-standard-high. At the press of a button the ratings and weights are applied and the Magic Quadrant is created! Well, that is how it would work in an ideal world. In reality, each vendor responds with different units, different time scales (oh, you meant calendar quarters!), and often just confusing entries. The analyst has to determine if the reported revenue is bookings, sales, or even if the vendor pulled some slight-of-hand reporting list price sales instead of discounted sales, or whether they bundle services and consulting into product revenue. It's a nightmare.

Once all the data is normalized and perhaps adjusted to reflect reality, an MQ is generated. Now comes the subjective part. The spreadsheet tool may cluster all the respective dots from all the vendors around the crosshairs—all the vendors are almost the same in ability to execute and completeness of vision. No problem, the scale is adjusted to spread them out. Then the analyst does a reality check. Does that vendor with the slick product but only 25 employees really belong in the Leaders Quadrant? Is IBM really a niche vendor in the space? How did the company that was first to market fall below the line into Visionary? How has the picture changed from the year before – can the major moves be explained?

After all the adjustments, and a review by the other analysts to get buy-in, the draft MQ is sent to all the participating vendors along with the brief synopsis of their company and product that will be in the main body of the research note. Then the fun begins. Every vendor who is not happy with their placement makes urgent requests for briefings to clarify their position or argue why they are so much better than the vendors ranked above them. Even the vendors placed in the Leaders Quadrant will not be happy unless they are the farthest UP and to the RIGHT. Every word of the synopsis will be scrutinized by the vendor and they will lobby for minor changes that portray them in a better light. Vendors have been known to count the number of words devoted to them and attempt to bring that number in line with their competitors' count.

Finally the analyst will complete the vendor response phase and send the MQ off to editing, where it is scrubbed for language compliance and formatted for publication. It is out of the analyst's hands. She breathes a sigh of relief and moves on to the other MQ for which she is responsible. Today an analyst may devote as much as 300 hours to creating and publishing a Magic Quadrant.

Jeff Pollard of Forrester provides insights on the volume of vendor-provided material Wave analysts need to read.

Forrester caps our character limits in vendor questionnaire responses to even the playing field, reduce redundancies, and to cut through fluffy marketing language. At the same time, this helps detect the most important and differentiating information about each product or service.

Unsurprisingly, a link exists between scores and word count. Vendors that reached the character count scored higher. We ask vendors to describe incredibly complex product and service capabilities in a limited number of words, and comprehensive answers take real estate. Those that scored 1s could not answer questions as thoroughly as their higher-scoring counterparts or tried to "tailor" answers to what they believed we were looking for. Between the two questionnaires submitted for the global and midsize Waves, we read over 100,000 words in total. To put this into perspective, the first two Harry Potter novels contain just over 76,000 and 85,000 words, respectively, and Harper Lee's classic To Kill a Mockingbird clocks in at 100,388.

In total, we spent 77 hours in externally facing parts of the Wave. Ninety-five hours went toward internal review.

In total, our research associate received 1,012 emails from our Wave participants for these two Waves: 626 in the global Wave and 386 from the midsize.

Alan Pelz-Sharpe covers another way an analyst tackles an evaluation report, and their focus on helping buyers.

I have been an analyst and commentator for many years now. For most of that time I have written or contributed to detailed, critical evaluations of software technologies. My audience is almost exclusively buyers and implementers of the technologies I cover, whose typical project sizes run into the high hundreds of thousands to the multiple millions. People read my research to create shortlists, and to give themselves a better chance of selecting the right product. It's a simple model really, much like a "Consumer Reports."

I play with the technologies, I see them in action, I talk to many users, I talk to channel partners, resellers, and also consultants and integrators. I also talk to the vendors, but more for fact checking, product demos, and gaining insights on nitpicky elements than anything else. I appreciate the help of vendors, but ultimately my research focuses on how products work and are sold in the real world, so the world of vendor marketing remains of peripheral interest.

Providing customers with honest and critical evaluations of products means highlighting all the warts, along with spotlighting all the shiny positives. If anything, my job is to focus on finding the warts. Let's be honest, it is not hard for a buyer to find the positives. They're deluged by "white papers," marketing collateral, and sales spin. Finding where a product's sweet spot or drawbacks reside is much harder.

It's my job to help buyers in that process, and if by definition that makes me unpopular at times among vendors, it still behooves AR people to work openly and professionally.

Roy Illsley gives us an inside view of the process to develop Omdia's Universe reports.

Omdia's Universe reports have a very transparent and detailed scoring process across many dimensions. It takes us about six months, plus a lot of vendor effort, so we only do them about every two years. We analyze detailed responses from the vendors, our trackers, and we partner with Trust Radius to provide customer feedback and sentiment on the vendor and the product.

We cover technologies as they get to the maturing stage and if they are interesting to users. For example, I'm doing one on AIOps next year, which will be the first one. I've written on the topic for a couple of years, but it won't be mature enough to be compared until next year. We have lightweight versions of the Universe, and sometimes – like in the case of Hyperconverged Infrastructure – we see little difference between the vendors so we need to do more depth to pull it out. On the other hand, in a mature market where this is little differentiation, we find less interest and drop it.

We determine the Universe reports among the analyst teams, but we have a feedback loop by confirming first with our subscribers. We want to make sure we produce the reports they are most interested in.

The outcome of these reports are quite valuable to vendors. They want to understand in more depth why they are where they are and what we recommend that they do. Those that aren't leaders want to know what they can do to become a leader… where the gaps are, where the market's heading, etc. It's interesting that just because a vendor is a leader, it doesn't mean they always will be. If the market's heading in a different direction and they have not changed, they will drop like a stone.

The outcome of these reports can surprise the analyst. We usually aren't surprised by the leader, but are surprised by some of the others in the leader's category. You don't dig in deeply enough in conversations to actually rate them. So it's only when you do this exercise that you fully understand what they are doing.

Handling evaluation reports takes an enormous amount of time and energy. As hard as it is for the vendor, it's even harder for the analyst. These are extremely demanding endeavors. The reports take months of scrutinizing mounds of product capabilities from a large field of vendors. There are briefings and demos. Analysts are under pressure. They have to produce a document that represents the players in a space, and they need to make judgments about who is hot and who is not. Those judgments affect buying decisions. These buying decisions affect vendors.

Analysts have to be confident and develop a thick skin that defends themselves from the wrath of vendors they judge unfavorably. Step into the analyst's shoes. It will give you a perspective that adds depth and dimension to the pixel-breaking work of vendor participation.

Conclusion

The analyst relations business is not for the faint hearted. It demands time, smarts, people skills, and an understanding of technology. The AR professional lives in a space where technology and people meet and sometimes differ, where expertise makes marketing difficult, where diplomacy is expected to make up for shortfalls in products or marketing. AR will always be a series of challenges and mysteries because AR is an art that encompasses multiple skill sets. As AR professionals, we are ambassadors, educators, strategists, messengers, therapists, technologists, and storytellers.

If there is one skill highlighted throughout this book, it is listening. Listen internally to your company's challenges. Listen to the analysts to understand how they can help. Listen to the individual analyst's needs. Listen to analyst's advice. Listen first and then apply what you hear.

Both the analyst and the vendor have a perspective, an attitude, a direction, a goal, a mindset. That is the world we live in, the orientation we come from. Sometimes we can't see the forest for the trees. When we step back and understand the individual analyst and see ourselves and our competitive environment through their eyes, we are better able to change the analysts, our company, and ourselves.

Listen to the analysts in this book. Listen to their wisdom. Their words provide a basis for your successful strategies. And then listen to the analysts you work with. Their words will guide you through your daily approach and will simplify your very complicated job.

Applying these learnings is where the real smarts comes in. Generic AR chops are a great foundation, but it is when you tailor your objectives and activities that your company flourishes. You are lauded for your contributions, you get a big raise. You smile with the feeling of great accomplishment. You thank the universe for landing in this crazy, always-moving, always-evolving space.

Afterword

Brian Sommer's ultimate guide to analyst archetypes

Assassin – This analyst has never met a vendor they liked, ever. They don't have much sympathy for vendor executives or the market, financial, product, etc. challenges before them. The Assassin takes pride in having never written a positive piece, ever.

Brand Builder/Destroyer – This analyst builds their personal brand up by destroying the brand of the vendor. They usually write tough pieces although these pieces don't have to be right or new. They just have to get ink for the analyst.

Curmudgeon – You could build an app that solved world hunger and the Curmudgeon would still find something to nitpick about. The Curmudgeon is not an Assassin as they are just always in a bad mood. This analyst can give praise but it often comes with some begrudging acceptance.

Egoist – Most analysts are really good but some see themselves in an especially rarefied light. These über-analysts make demands on vendors that make riders in rock star contracts look tame. These folks only stay at the 5+star hotels (if they even exist), always get the vendor to provide them a limo to/from the airport, fly them first class, etc. I guess all the rest of us working-stiff analysts should be happy that we sometimes get to periodically co-exist in the egocentric world of these most special people. (Yeah, right!)

Fish out of water – This is someone who has hung out an analyst shingle but never did technology implementations. They might bluff well but their lack of experience eventually shines through. As analysts go, they're usually short-lived and their inexperience is quickly apparent.

Frustrated Politician – Some analysts really want to change the world. To that end, they mix technology and their far-right or far-left politics into their writings. If you're not on their page politically, your technology may not be on their top picks list.

Newbie – This analyst usually says nothing the whole day although some mistakenly chirp up and get eviscerated by other analysts – That's never a pretty sight. They can go from newbie to roadkill in a single bad question.

Note Taker – A note taker just states or re-states what the vendor says. They add little or no other insight. Generally, they are not very helpful for most readers but can be a darling of many vendors, especially those that want to control the message in the market.

Purist/Theoretician/Professor – This analyst can debate the arcane, immaterial and theoretical to death. They have a deeply rooted opinion about a subject and are waiting for a chance to tangle with some vendor executive to see whose command of the subject reigns supreme.

Rifleman – To be honest, this is a role I relish but others are very good at this, too. This is the analyst that finds the shortest distance between hype and reality (or non-news and wishful posturing). These folks call bulls**t every time it tries to rear its ugly head. This is the analyst that keeps vendors honest. When they draw first blood, then the other analysts pounce. When that many analysts pounce, it's like a National Geographic episode on piranha attacks (i.e., not for the faint of heart).

Ryan Seacrest (with apologies to the real Ryan Seacrest) – This analyst is always positive to the star vendors in the industry. This analyst type is always full of fawning, gushy 'reporting'. They speak of vendor news items (e.g., the new tax table update in version 10.5.3.A41.6 of an old fixed assets application) with all the 'exclusive' hype usually accorded a Kardashian engagement rumor.

Salesperson – Somehow, this 'analyst' always manages to mention that they have a template, framework, project, white paper, etc. that the vendor can license. I've heard some of these pitches enough times to sell the solution myself.

Same Question Every Year – This analyst has 1-3 questions and asks them at every vendor confab. They ask these same questions year in/out. They are an old fashioned vinyl LP that has a scratch on it that makes it repeat the same groove indefinitely.

SBD (silent by deadly) – There are actually lots of these analysts. These analysts sit through entire days of briefings without uttering a word. Then, when they're headed to the airport they post an atom bomb of a report.

Snark – The Snark sends out a few Tweets per event but each one is a tongue-in-cheek jewel (e.g., "What's the difference between Vendor XYZ and a bowl of yogurt? Only one of these has a good culture!") . These are the analysts whose short pithy stuff everyone loves to read. They're entertaining but may not deliver the longer, in-depth reviews.

Still beat your wife? – This analyst spends hours perfecting the most impossible questions for vendor executives to answer without coming off badly. These are the questions the vendor's PR team has tried to prepare executives for and hopefully, they won't take the bait.

Unmovable Object – This analyst has an opinion that no amount of facts will convince otherwise. He/She takes stubborn to all new levels. They steadfastly maintain their viewpoint no matter how many others have already weighed in on the inaccuracy of it.

Volumizer – This analyst sends 60-300 tweets per briefing along with 4-6 blog posts per hour. I'm never sure what they actually capture during the event but analysts like me often find our questions/comments in their content. Personally, I like that they help promote my brand.

Reprinted with permission by ZDNet.

Contributor Directory

Robin Bloor
Bloor is the founder of Bloor Research and covers a variety of technology topics from eCommerce through to IT strategy and trends.

https://sag.cx/C

Anton Chuvakin
Chuvakin was a Research VP and Distinguished Analyst at Gartner covering a broad range of security operations and detection and response topics.

https://sag.cx/D

Lawrence Gasman
Gasman founded Inside Quantum Technology. He has been tracking commercialization of new technologies for 35 years and has written four books.

https://sag.cx/E

James Governor
Governor is founder of RedMonk and focuses on developers as the real key influencers in tech. An ex-journalist, he has managed teams and news agendas in weekly publication grind. IBM and MS watcher since 1995.

https://sag.cx/G

Mike Guay
Guay is a former Gartner analyst focusing on enterprise applications. He has more than 30 years experience with a variety of organizations from large multi-billion dollar, multi-national defense contractors, to start-up technology firms, to public sector entities.

https://sag.cx/H

Rachel Happe
Happe is a former analyst at IDC, covering social media and online advertising technology platforms. She is currently the co-founder of The Community Roundtable, which is dedicated to advancing the business of community.

https://sag.cx/J

Roy Illsley
Illsley is the Chief Analyst at Omdia and has more than 35 years' IT experience. He specializes in virtualization and cloud computing.

https://sag.cx/L

Ritu Jyoti
Jyoti covers Artificial Intelligence (AI) strategies at IDC She focuses on the state of enterprise AI efforts, organizational impact and she provides guidance on building new capabilities and prioritization of investment options.

https://sag.cx/M

Charlene Li
Li founded Altimeter Research and was a former analyst at Forrester. She is an expert on digital transformation, leadership, customer experience and the future of work. She has authored six books, including the New York Times bestseller "Open Leadership."

https://sag.cx/N

Rebecca Lieb
Lieb is a co-founder at Kaleido Insights and is focused on Marketing, Content, Media, and the relationship between organizations and their market.

https://sag.cx/O

Kevin Lucas
Lucas is a leading expert on analyst relations at Forrester and addresses AR's strategic value and objectives to help AR teams deliver that value.

https://sag.cx/P

Laurie McCabe
McCabe founded SMB Group and has more than 20 years of experience in the IT industry. She covers the small and medium business (SMB) market in cloud computing, mobile solutions, business solutions, social networking and collaboration, and managed services.

https://sag.cx/Q

Henry Morris
Morris, a long time analyst from IDC, researches and writes on the subject of analytics - its application in business, and the need for ethical controls and governance of intelligent systems.

https://sag.cx/R

Wendy Nather
Nather has been a research director covering enterprise security for 451 Research. She has 30+ years' technical experience in IT operations and security, including twelve years in the financial services industry and five years in state government.

https://sag.cx/S

Daniel Newman
Newman founded Futurum Research and explores Digital Transformation and how it is influencing the enterprise.

https://sag.cx/T

Stephen O'Grady
O'Grady co-founded RedMonk and helps companies understand and work with developers.

https://sag.cx/U

Peter O'Neill
O'Neill, former Gartner analyst, advises IT vendor and end user clients and performs research-based consulting. He combines strong research capabilities with comparative vendor assessments and actionable advice.

https://sag.cx/V

Jeremiah Owyang
Owyang, former Forrester analyst, founded Kaleido Insights and covers how new technologies impact business models and how corporations must innovate.

https://sag.cx/W

Bob Parker
Parker is a senior vice president at IDC, responsible for the global industry research teams covering verticals, emerging topics, enterprise applications, and data intelligence.

https://sag.cx/X

Alan Pelz-Sharpe
Pelz-Sharpe, founder of Deep Analysis, focuses on technologies like AI/ML/RPA and Blockchain and helps make them explainable and actionable.

https://sag.cx/Y

Chris Perrine
Perrine is VP, APAC for G2. He has been in sales and marketing for Forrester, IDC, and Springboard Research.

https://sag.cx/Z

Jeff Pollard
Pollard is an Forrester analyst who covers the role of the CISO, specializing in topics related to security strategy, budgets, metrics, business cases, and presenting to the board.

https://sag.cx/AA

Mark Smith
Smith founded Ventana Research and is an expert in enterprise software and business technology innovations including business analytics, big data, cloud computing, business collaboration, mobile technology and social media.

https://sag.cx/AB

Brian Sommer

Sommer, founder of TechVentive, is an industry influencer in the ERP, Finance and Human Resources markets. He has a unique mixture of serious technology expertise, experience with Fortune 500 firms, and a strong marketing background.

https://sag.cx/AC

Richard Stiennon

Stiennon, former Gartner analyst, is the author of several books, most recently, Curmudgeon, on how to be an analyst. He is the Chief Research Analyst at IT-Harvest and covers the security market.

https://sag.cx/AD

John Sumser

Sumser is a principal analyst at HRExaminer. He explores the people, technology, ideas and careers of senior leaders in human resources and human capital.

https://sag.cx/AE

Jon Toigo

Toigo, who died in 2019, was a major analyst in the database storage space. Jon was founder and chairman of Toigo Partners International, and the Data Management Institute. He was a great writer and we are delighted to include his thoughts.

https://sag.cx/AF

Rik Turner

Turner, principal analyst at Omdia, specializes in cybersecurity technology trends, IT security, compliance, and call recording.

https://sag.cx/AG

Ray Wang

Wang is the principal analyst and founder of Constellation Research and a major technology industry influencer. He covers disruptive technologies and new business models impacting the enterprise.

https://sag.cx/AH

David Wilson

Wilson is founder of Fosway Group, leading research, analysis and insight for next generation HR, talent and learning.

https://sag.cx/AI

Josh Zelonis

Zelonis, former Forrester analyst covering threat detection and response, specializes in enterprise security strategy, adversarial tactics, and defensive technologies.

https://sag.cx/AJ

Find out more

ROBIN SCHAFFER guides analyst and influencer relations teams in strategy, execution and value creation. She has led transformative analyst relations and marketing leadership for three decades. Her prior experience in the technology industry includes Unit4, NICE Systems, and AT&T.

She graduated Summa Cum Laude from William Paterson University of New Jersey with a bachelor's degree in English.

DR. EFREM MALLACH has been involved in analyst relations since the late 1970s, when he represented Honeywell to the then-nascent industry analyst community. Since 1987, when he wrote the first book on Industry Analyst Relations, 'Win them Over', he has held leading roles in AR consultancies: Kensington Group, Lighthouse Analyst Relations and Kea Company.

He has a PhD from the Sloan School of Management at the Massachusetts Institute of Technology.

SAGECIRCLE™ helps analyst relations (AR) teams to focus on business value. They take clients from static "best practices" to innovative thinking that leverages insights, drives revenue and builds brand value.

The team brings together AR domain expertise, years of experience in the analyst game as end-users, analysts, AR researchers and vendors, and new insights from working with some of the most dynamic AR professionals. They work with global technology vendors to transform analyst relations by accelerating sales pipelines, implementing business strategy and generating intelligence.

SageCircle is a member of the Kea Company Group.

CPSIA information can be obtained
at www.ICGtesting.com
Printed in the USA
BVHW040522201220
596114BV00017B/645